PS
1097
Z 5
G 7   Grattan, C, Hartley
        Bitter Bierce

17256

DATE DUE			
DEC 7 70			
OCT 2 2 1975			
NOV 1 9 1975			
Dec. 17			
DEC. 8 '81			
DEC 1 9 1980			
OCT 2 9 1980			
MAR 04 1988			
APR 02 1988			
MAY 2 2 1992			
MAY 1 7 1993			

BITTER BIERCE

BITTER BIERCE

A Mystery of American Letters

BY

C. HARTLEY GRATTAN

My! how my fame rings out in every zone—
A thousand critics shouting: "He's unknown!"

AMBROSE BIERCE

COOPER SQUARE PUBLISHERS, INC.

NEW YORK
1966

To
L. G. and L. G.

Published 1966 by
Cooper Square Publishers, Inc.
59 Fourth Avenue, New York, N. Y. 10003
Library of Congress Catalog Card Number: 66-24261

PRINTED IN THE UNITED STATES OF AMERICA
by SENTRY PRESS, NEW YORK, N. Y. 10019

PREFACE

THE principal thing I had in mind while working on this book was to write as interestingly as possible about Ambrose Bierce. It was my purpose to make him better known and better understood. Unfortunately I soon discovered that there were obstacles in the way of making this a definitive biography. The critical discussion could not, of course, claim to be definitive in any case. The information about Bierce is extremely scanty, and it is very difficult to increase it by writing to people who are alleged to have known Bierce intimately. Most of them, on investigation, turn out to be persons who have met Bierce on some stray occasion, or persons who in conversation have shown a more intimate knowledge of his career than the general, but that is not to say that they know more than the diligent student can discover. There is a good deal of gossip about Bierce floating around, and, of course, it must be used with caution and labelled gossip when it is committed to print. Nevertheless, various persons have helped me materially, and I acknowledge that assistance below.

I have deliberately chosen to be exceedingly matter of fact. I have also chosen to make use of a device that is associated in the public mind with exceeding dullness: I have used footnotes freely in the biographical section and occasionally elsewhere. I have thought it necessary to resort to footnotes in the biography for the reason that it is the first attempt to write an inclusive sketch of Bierce's life and I wanted to let future students know where I obtained my information. I also realize that a good many of the things I have to say will be denied by partisans of Bierce, and I wanted to forestall unnecessary correspondence about such matters. The footnotes give my authorities, and those who are disposed to quarrel may quarrel with my authorities as much as they please. On the other hand,

if this book comes to the attention of anyone
who can add to the information about Bierce,
I shall be only too glad to receive such information for incorporation in later editions, if
any.

There is a difficulty with which all students
of Bierce's mental development must deal.
There are no records that show him growing
up to the ideas that he eventually entertained. We have him as a finished product.
Even when, in the *Collected Edition*, the essays
are dated, it assists us very little to observe
the dates, for the fact that he preserved the
essays indicates that they represent his mature opinions on some subject. If he had grown
out of the opinions he would not have made
them permanently available. Since we cannot trace his mental growth it is difficult to
say much about the origin of his ideas. I have
pointed out in several places that Bierce did
not buttress his essays with scholarship. We
find an astonishing lack of reference to other
writers and thinkers. Consequently one can
only guess to what thinkers he was indebted.

I have chosen not to guess too frequently. Others may not be so modest. I have, however, thought it not entirely impertinent to cast doubts upon the extent and depth of Bierce's scholarship, and I have ventured an explanation for its lack of extent and depth.

I am indebted to the Book Club of California (Mr. Oscar Lewis, Secretary) for permission to quote freely from its edition of Bierce's letters; to Mr. Samuel Loveman (with whom I had an interesting conversation about Bierce) for permission to quote from the correspondence with Bierce that he published in *Twenty-One Letters of Ambrose Bierce;* and to A. & C. Boni, Inc., for permission to quote from Bierce's *Collected Works.* It is necessary to note here that Mrs. Helen Bierce Isgrigg has issued a warning that she will not tolerate the printing of any of her father's letters. There are, consequently, no letters by Bierce cited in this volume that have not been published before. My lawyer assures me that these letters are outside of Mrs. Isgrigg's control. I owe a great deal to the writings of George

Sterling that deal with Bierce. I am grateful to the writers of the various essays, in magazines and books, that I have read in my search for information about Bierce and for insight into his personality and work. I read with great interest Mr. Vincent Starrett's all too brief pamphlet. I am indebted to Messrs. E. D. Coblentz, Robert Davis, Edward H. Hamilton, and Robert Howe.Fletcher for information communicated to me in letters. I am especially indebted to my friend Mr. John Francis O'Brien for investigating the records of the Adjutant General's Office with the result cited in the text. I wish to thank Mr. Clay Kennedy for his assistance. And I am tremendously indebted to my wife for restraining my impatience when I felt that this monograph was going to end abruptly up some blind alley.

C. H. G.

New York City,
October 1, 1928.

CONTENTS

PART I
BIOGRAPHICAL

I never read biographical "stuff" of other writers—and think it beside the question. Moreover, it is distinctly mischievous to letters. It throws no light on one's work, but on the contrary "darkens counsel." —Ambrose Bierce, in a letter dated November 29, 1892.

O F ALL the writers who did their most substantial work between the close of the Civil War and 1900 Ambrose Bierce was the only one who carried on an active, open, uncompromising war with the environment that was oppressive to them all. Henry and William James, Mark Twain, Howells, Bret Harte, John Burroughs, all compromised in their various ways. Hamlin Garland and Frank Norris started out bravely enough but gave up after a while. Sidney Lanier and William Vaughn Moody revolted incidentally. Most of the popular writers did not even know there was anything to criticize. They were dead from the beginning. Instead of, like Mark Twain, expressing his protest by indirection (as with *Huckleberry Finn* and *Life on the Mississippi*) or posthumously (as in *What Is Man* and *The Mysterious Stranger*), Bierce was out in the open from the beginning. He made a business of cracking skulls and ideas. Product of three disillusioning experiences, pioneer life, war, and journalistic uproars, he ended up with almost nothing that he could regard as sacred. He was an all-inclusive cynic.

So many of Bierce's incidental ideas are held by the commonalty to-day that a detailed rehearsal of what he thought may occasionally skirt closely upon the domain of platitude. His fundamental ideas have no more adherents to-day than when he announced them. His art continues to be quite generally falsely evaluated. It has been Bierce's misfortune that while his ideas have gone into the common stock of most thinking men, his name has been detached from them, and so his credit as an originator is small. This is highly unfortunate, for men of little originality can to-day pass as smart by parroting ideas that Bierce developed and expressed between 1881 and 1905. What his perverse thinking cost him is only too well known. Chief among his payments for thinking acutely in an age hostile to the exercise of the critical intelligence—let alone the cynical intelligence—were unpopularity and obscurity. He took what joy he could out of his "notoriety as an obscurian." He knew that the world was under no obligation to pay him the tribute he felt he deserved.

It has not been his fortune to achieve, either, the stable posthumous reputation upon which he banked with considerable confidence. His position in American letters is still a matter of debate. Lesser men than he have been given a permanent niche, but it is doubtful that it would cause any widespread comment if a history of American literature were published to-morrow entirely omitting his name. For example, there are two volumes on the shelves behind me that are fairly representative inclusive surveys of modern American writers. The first is *American and British Literature Since 1890* (1925) by Carl and Mark Van Doren. Bierce is nowhere mentioned, but James Whitcomb Riley, Richard Hovey, O. Henry, and George Ade are. The second is Dr.

BITTER BIERCE

F. L. Pattee's *American Literature Since 1870*
(1922), a standard reference work. It disposes
of Bierce in seventeen lines. The judgment is
adverse. In all fairness to Dr. Pattee, however,
it may be pointed out that in *The Development
of the American Short Story* (1923) he pro-
nounces the fairest academic judgment that I
know, with the exception of that of Dr. P. H.
Boynton in *More Contemporary Americans*:
"The man was an artist, cold, cynical, conscious of his art. He was not bound by rules:
he was heedless sometimes even of fundamentals. . . . Artificial as was the material in
which he worked, and deliberate and ironic
as were his motifs, nevertheless he was able to
create situations hauntingly suggestive. Many
of his stories begin for the reader where the
last sentence ends. His ghost stories, totally
unexplained, recorded with circumstances of
actual history, nevertheless have within them
suggestions of an abnormal psychological
world, possible within each of us, and those
more terrifying than even a supernatural ap-

6

parition. It is the last touch of art: it is the art that compels the reader to search his own soul." The discrepancy between this judgment and that of the previous year is inexplicable.

But still Bierce is not generally read. His complete works will never be widely read, and there is no good reason why they should be. It is a genuine misfortune, however, that most readers are content to stop after reading his war and ghost stories. They are not the whole of Bierce. He was a man of ideas. As a wit and satirist he perhaps outranks every other American writer. He wrote political and social criticism of a high order. He is well worth considering, even, as a literary critic and as a poet. Joseph Conrad complained that he was tired of being called a "novelist of the sea." Why not, with equal justice, he asked, call Thomas Hardy a "novelist of the land"? Ambrose Bierce's ghost has every reason to complain of his being known exclusively as a writer about war and the supernatural.

BITTER BIERCE

It is difficult to improve upon Bierce's own description of his position. He is a notorious obscurian. His reputation, as Arnold Bennett has said, is underground. But it is healthy and it will grow. Bierce will establish himself in a secure position in the living American tradition. Once achieved, the position will never be lost. The core of Bierce's work is too solid to be entirely eroded by time.

It is far from customary to associate Ambrose Bierce with William Dean Howells, but that is because it has been overlooked that they both came from the same state and lived in it at about the same time. Bierce was born at Pomery, Meiggs County[1], Ohio, on June 24, 1842, and Howells at Martin's Ferry, Belmont

---

[1]It is sometimes said that Bierce was born in Guernsey County. He laid this rumour to rest in characteristic fashion. He sent a correspondent a clipping which read: "In Guernsey County, Ohio, more than a half century ago, there is said to have been a heavy shower of stones that caused many to believe that the world was coming to an end." His comment was: "I fancy that *this* is what gave your friend the impression that I once lived in Guernsey County, Ohio. He assumed that when God was throwing stones I would be the natural target." Cf. "Mr. Boythorn-Bierce," by Ruth Guthrie Harding, *Bookman*, August, 1925.

County, on March 1, 1837. Both, too, were early associated with printing. It was their introduction to literature. Both were prevented from getting an orderly education, but both utilized to the full the meagre resources at their command. It is illuminating to bring them together in this fashion, for they diverged to the opposite poles of the literary compass. Bierce absorbed all the American experience at his command. He enlisted in the Civil War as a private. Howells took the opportunity to spend the war years in Italy. At the close of the war Howells settled in New York and finally established himself in Boston, the literary centre of the nation. Bierce gravitated to the opposite side of the continent, to San Francisco, where all was rough and ready and literature was a rare concern. Howells became the most powerful literary influence of his day; Bierce never commanded a public of any magnitude. Howells accepted his environment and allowed it to dominate him; Bierce rejected his environment and trampled on it so far as he could.

BITTER BIERCE

Howells was crippled by acceptance; Bierce by rejection.

Bierce was one of twelve children each having a name beginning with A: Abigail, Addison, Aurelius, Amelia, Ann, Augustus, Andrew, Almeda, Albert, and Ambrose. The other two died in infancy. His father was Marcus Aurelius Bierce and his mother's maiden name was Laura Sherwood. Bierce was christened Ambrose Gwinnett, and he liked neither name to excess. He confessed that Ambrose was only pleasing to him when spoken by a woman, and he concealed the Gwinnett with an initial until he finally dropped it altogether. The dropping of the G from his signature is of particular interest, for it is one of the few acknowledgments he ever made that an enemy in controversy had made a hit. He had roasted an erstwhile friend, Arthur McEwen, in the columns of the San Francisco *Examiner*, and McEwen in his reply called him, in parody on his initials, Almighty God Bierce. It seems that this was so hard a slap that Bierce immediately ceased to use the G.

Marcus Aurelius Bierce was a farmer who succeeded in making little more than a living. He had two brothers who achieved at least passing note in the world. One became a colonel in the Northern army during the Civil War, Colonel Royal C. Bierce, and the other, Frederick, was concerned in the founding of Rush Medical School, now part of the University of Chicago. The Bierce family was of New England origin and emigrated to Ohio in the days when it was still called Western Reserve. They were solid Congregationalists and contributed their share to the establishment of Puritanism in the Ohio Valley. By his ferocious onslaughts on the faith of his fathers, religious and moral, Bierce became a sort of family black sheep. Bierce never expressed any particular regard for his father and never, so far as written records go, spoke of his mother. On one occasion he informed a friend that his father was too poor to provide him with more than an extremely elementary education. Bierce, senior, however, seems to have been something of a reader, for his library was rather extensive, and in it Ambrose laid the foundations of his later literary taste and prejudice. "My father was a poor farmer and could give me no general education, but he had a good library, and to his books I owe all that I have."[2] When he was but ten years old he read Pope's version of Homer.

Ambrose was very young when the family left Meiggs County and went to live in Elkhart, Indiana. It was there that he grew up and that most of the family lived out their lives. Little is known about his brothers and sisters. His favourite brother, Albert, preceded him to San Francisco and indeed drew Ambrose there for permanent residence after the war. He was employed in the mint. In his letters Bierce usually referred to him affectionately as "Old Grizzly." Yet Bierce said

[2]Unless otherwise noted, all quotations from letters are from *The Letters of Ambrose Bierce*, edited by B. C. Pope and published by the California Book Club. They are quoted by express permission.

flatly that Albert was "not 'fully cognizant' of [his] history, anyhow not of the part that is interesting." And shortly before he went to Mexico in 1913 Bierce wrote his brother such a scurrilous letter that George Sterling believes it helped to bring on Albert's death shortly thereafter. A second brother, Andrew, spent all of his life on a farm near Elkhart. He seems not to have been overly brilliant, for he rejoiced in the unflattering nickname of "Dime." In his old age he had but a vague remembrance of Ambrose. A sister, Abigail, is said to have died a missionary in Africa. Bierce's parents lived out their lives in Elkhart but are buried in Warsaw, Indiana, the birthplace of Theodore Dreiser.

Beyond a fondness for reading, Bierce's boyhood was that of an ordinary poor boy. A schoolmate has written: "The boy had what was called a poor chance. He quit school early and went to work in the brickyards. He graduated there in due time, and came downtown to work. Andrew Faber was running an establishment on Main Street in those days, a bakery-grocery-restaurant-saloon, and he took Ambrose on as all-around handy man. When the boys got together to play cards to see who'd treat, it was Ambrose Bierce who brought the beer and sandwiches. . . . He was always rather queer and different."[3]

Sometime after the period of this bit of reminiscence Bierce must have learned the trade of printer, for he gave that as his occupation when he enlisted in the Union Army for service in the Civil War. The war gave him his chance. He entered it an ill-educated farm boy and he emerged from it intellectually mature and full of a desire to be a writer, if we are to believe Albert. It is characteristic of Bierce that in later life he lost all belief in the issues of the Civil War, if indeed they ever meant anything to him. "They found," he wrote in a letter of 1903, "a Confederate soldier over there [the other side of a mountain on which

[3]Quoted from the Elkhart *Truth* in the *American Mercury*, July, 1925, p. xxii.

he was spending his summer vacation] the other day, with his rifle alongside. I'm going over to beg his pardon." His nostalgia for the war days in later life, which was recurrent, was compounded of recollections of camp life, battle, and military manœuvres. It had nothing to do with patriotism. It is alleged that he enlisted as a drummer boy. In any case, he entered the ranks at La Porte, Indiana, on September 5, 1861, and became a member of Company C of the Ninth Indiana Infantry. He was mustered out, with the rank of first lieutenant, at Huntsville, Louisiana, on February 16, 1865.[4]

Most of his service in the war was with the army of the Cumberland. He soon distin-

---

[4]It is asserted again and again in accounts of Bierce that he was breveted major by special act of Congress at the close of the war. If so there is no note to that effect in the records of the Adjutant General's Office which were investigated for me by my friend John F. O'Brien. Mr. O'Brien, a lawyer in the employ of the government, writes on the point: "The appointing power of men in the military and naval forces is now solely in the President. Since the basis of the doctrine is the Constitution, the same rule probably was in full force during the Civil War. The most Congress could do is to authorize the appointment." I should be happy if someone can clear up this mystery.

guished himself and was attached to the head-
quarters staff (particularly to the staff of
General W. B. Hazen) as a topographical
engineer. Where he picked up the training
necessary for this special sort of work I do not
know. He remembered the war with pleasure all
of his days and undoubtedly regarded it as the
most interesting and satisfactory part of his life.
Not only did he return to the war for material
for his short stories, but he retained an abiding
interest in military tactics and the art of war
in general. His interest in war was the determining factor in the final adventure of his life.
As a topographical engineer he was bound to
engage in many hazardous exploits. Among
the major engagements in which he took
part were Chickamauga, Shiloh, Murfreesboro,
Kenesaw Mountain, Franklin, and Nashville.
His reminiscences of the war years (contained
in his *Collected Works*, Volume I) are charac-
teristically impersonal but vivid. A better idea
of his reaction to the war can be obtained from
his fiction.

BITTER BIERCE

Bierce was twice wounded during the war. On the first occasion he was but slightly hurt, in the foot. At Kenesaw Mountain, however, he received a severe wound in the head which necessitated his being invalided home for three months. According to his brother Albert, this wound completely changed Bierce's character. Commenting on it years later, Albert said: "He was never the same after that. Some of the iron of that shell seemed to stick in his brain, and he became bitter and suspicious, especially of his close friends. He would remember each failing and slight, fancied or otherwise, of such persons, say nothing of it at the time, and then, many years afterward, release the stored-up poison in a flood."[5] While invalided home Bierce showed how deep seated his interest in literature was, for he read a poem to which he referred George Sterling years after, in the *Atlantic Monthly*. His misfortune also gave those members of the

---

[5] Quoted by George Sterling, "The Shadow Maker," the *American Mercury*, October, 1925.

family who remained in Indiana their last
glimpse of him. He visited the farm of his
brother Andrew: "'I don't remember much
about Ambrose. The last I saw of him was
during the Civil War. Once when he was
wounded he came home on furlough,' and
Mrs. Bierce finishes the story: 'We were on
the farm, and Ambrose rode out on a horse.
He had his head tied up, where he'd been shot.
When he rode away on the horse, it was the
last we saw of him.'" It was after this episode
that, through his own foolhardiness, he was
captured, but he was fortunate enough quickly
to make his escape.

The war over, Bierce went through a period
of indecision. He considered remaining in the
regular army. He thought of joining his brother
Albert in San Francisco, which was eventually
his course, but it was arrived at indirectly.
His first postwar occupation was in Alabama,
where he went as an official of the Treasury
Department. He served as collector and cus-
todian of "captured and abandoned property,"

chiefly cotton. The following year he made the journey across the plains from Omaha, Nebraska, to Dutch Flat, California. He was, in his own words, "an engineer *attaché* to an expedition through Dakota and Montana, to inspect some new military posts. The expedition consisted, where the Indians preserved the peace, of the late General W. B. Hazen, myself, a cook, and teamster; elsewhere we had an escort of cavalry. My duty, as I was given to understand it, was to amuse the general and other large game, make myself as comfortable as possible without too much discomfort to others, and when in an unknown country, survey and map our route for the benefit of those who might come after. By a master stroke of military humor we were ordered to return [to Washington] via Salt Lake City, San Francisco, and Panama. I obeyed until I got as far as San Francisco, where, finding myself appointed to a second lieutenancy in the Regular Army, ingratitude, more strong than traitors' arms, vanquished me. I resigned, parted from Hazen more in sorrow than in anger and remained in California."[6]

He found employment in the mint with his brother. He soon began to contribute to the newspapers. According to his own confession he was a bad writer at this period. "I was a slovenly writer in those days though enough better than my neighbours to have attracted my own attention. My knowledge of English was imperfect 'a whole lot.' Indeed, my intellectual status (whatever it may be, and God knows it's enough to make me blush) was of slow growth—as was my moral. I mean, I had not literary sincerity." In any case, he was sufficiently good to stand out from among his fellows and to be appointed editor of the *News-Letter*. Shortly after, he was married. The exact date is uncertain.[7] Probably nothing contributed more to his subsequent black view of life than the miserable failure of his family affairs, nor could the outcome of his venture

[6]Cf. "Bits of Autobiography," in *Collected Works*, Vol. I.
[7]The fact is from a letter to me from E. H. Hamilton of San Francisco.

well have been farther from his undoubted expectations. Previous to his marriage Bierce had lost a sweetheart to a socialist, and both George Sterling and Upton Sinclair attribute his abnormal hatred of socialists and socialism to this happening. It illustrates, also, the fact that Bierce's constant war on the emotions was a reflex of his own extreme emotional sensitivity. The woman he finally won was Mollie Day, described as the reigning beauty of San Francisco society. They were married at the home of Judge Noble Hamilton at San Leandro.[8] Apparently the marriage was short-lived, for the friends of his second San Francisco period always refer to him as long separated from his wife. Once separated they never met again. Three children were born to the couple, Helen, who is still living, Day, who was killed in a drunken argument over a woman in northern California, and Leigh, who died (March 31, 1901) in New York City,

[8]The fact is from a letter to me from E. H. Hamilton of San Francisco.

where he was working as a newspaper man.[9] The latter, like his elder brother, was extremely headstrong. When he was but a lad his father found him to be entangled with a young woman, a connection that Leigh obstinately refused to break off. Finally, and apparently in desperation, Bierce talked to his son with more than usual severity and brought him to reason by recounting some happenings in his own life. What these happenings were is unknown, but when the relation was over Leigh Bierce, shaken emotionally, burst into George Sterling's rooms and said with intense feeling, "My father is a greater man than Christ. He has suffered more than Christ."[10] Any statement about what it was that Bierce told his son must be purely speculative, but I have a notion that it referred to his unfortunate married life. No motive has ever been assigned to his sudden determination to go to London.

---

[9]A memorial to Leigh Bierce is the story, "John Mortonson's Funeral," in his father's *Can Such Things Be?*

[10]This episode is variously related but it apparently originated with Sterling.

Again, I think, we must return to his marriage. Though all witnesses agree that he was early estranged from his wife, none has attempted to say why or how. In his sudden departure for London, he was undoubtedly seeking to obliterate the memory of his marital unhappiness. That he never succeeded in doing so is obvious, and that it coloured his whole life is beyond doubt.

He went to London in 1871, and it was there that he really learned his trade as a writer and published his first books. He apparently always entertained the notion that in England one would find the fountainhead of Anglo-Saxon culture. It is notable that he passed by New York and Boston without pausing. In any case, his admiration for the English was deep seated and long enduring. No modern Anglomaniac has been more persistent in paying tribute to the English tradition of life and letters.

In London, Bierce associated himself with the group that centred about *Fun,* which was edited by Tom Hood the younger. This group included such figures as George Augustus Sala, Mayne Reid, W. S. Gilbert, and George R. Sims. Although Bierce claims intimate association with these figures, none of them has left any extensive written records of the acquaintance. What has chiefly survived is a series of anecdotes the most famous of which is that of Bierce's relations with John Camden Hotten. When Bierce arrived in London he carried with him a collection of clippings of his California work. One day at the Unity Club John Thompson, who had been Swinburne's secretary, saw them and remarked, "My boy, Hotten will jump at them." Hotten had introduced Bret Harte and John Hay into England. Apparently Hotten jumped, for in 1873 there appeared two selections from this material, *Nuggets and Dust* and *The Fiend's Delight*. The material in the latter was highly various and was classified under the headings, "Some Fiction," "Tall Talk," "Current Journalings," "Laughorisms," "Musings," and

"Poesy." W. S. Gilbert did a title-page illustration. In addition it carried a preface which read in part: "The atrocities constituting this 'cold collation' of diabolisms are taken mainly from various Californian journals. They are cast in the American language, and liberally enriched with unintelligibility. If they should prove incomprehensible on this side of the Atlantic, the reader can pass to the other side at a moderately extortionate charge. In the pursuit of my design I think I have killed a good many people in one way or another; but the reader will please to observe that they were not people worth the trouble of leaving alive. Besides, I had the interests of my collaborator to consult. In writing, as in compiling, I have been ably assisted by my scholarly friend, Mr. Satan, and to this worthy gentleman must be attributed most of the views herein set forth. While the plan of the work is partly my own, its spirit is wholly his; and this illustrates the ascendency of the creative over the merely imitative mind. *Palmam qui meruit ferat*—I shall be content with the profit."[11]

Hotten was notoriously poor pay, and he served Bierce in his usual fashion. Bierce succeeded in getting a check from him by dint of constant dunning, but it was postdated, and before it was due Hotten died. Bierce heard of his death and started for the bank hoping to beat the news, but evil fate led him to stop at a taproom frequented by his friends. He stopped too long, and the news got to the bank, and he lost his money. Sala, however, on this occasion composed the famous epitaph:

> Hotten
> Rotten
> Forgotten.

Posterity, at least, is compensated.

For the year previous to this outburst of book publication, Bierce had been a somewhat regular contributor to *Fun*. His contributions

---

[11]Quoted by Walter Jerrold in "The Identity of Dod Grile," London *Bookman*, June, 1921. Mr. Jerrold notes that Bierce drew on these books for his *Collected Works* as follows: Fables in Vol. IV; some epigrams in Vol. VIII; and some of the "tangential views" in Vol. IX.

took the form of "The Fables of Zambi the Parsee" and misspelled zoölogy essays, the latter in a tradition established by Thackeray in his "Memoirs of C. J. Yellowplush" and the "Diary of C. Jeames de la Pluche," and taken up and run into the ground by a whole group of minor American humorists. The first series of fables ran from July 13th to September 28th. On November 16th Bierce contributed a fable in verse and on November 23d resumed his regular contribution of a prose fable. All of his work was done under the pen name, "Dod Grile." His London books were signed in that fashion also. In addition to his contributions to *Fun* he also wrote for Tom Hood's *Comic Annual* for 1873 and again in 1874. The first contribution was a skit entitled "How I Came to Like Dogs" and is written in a vein of absurd exaggeration. Curiously enough, while the writer consistently refers to himself as Mr. Grile in the text, it is signed A. G. Bierce. For 1874 he wrote a short bit entitled "Curried Cow," also in an exaggerated manner. It was signed Dod Grile. In 1874 a book of selections from his *Fun* stuff was published under the title *Cobwebs from an Empty Skull*. In later years Bierce preferred to ignore all three of these books, although he drew upon them for his collected works.[12] He even cast a cloud over their birth and definitely frowned on any project to reprint them: "It is a matter of no great importance to me, but the republication of the foolish books that you mention would not be agreeable to me. They have no merit or interest. One of them, *The Fiend's Delight*, was published against my protest; the utmost concession that the compiler and publisher (the late J. C. Hotten of London) would make was to let me edit his collection of my stuff and write a preface." (October 29, 1907.)

Bierce also contributed to various forgotten humorous journals, most of them edited by

---

[12]During his active writing life, Bierce was frequently critical of the product of an earlier period. It is indeed curious that he sunk his powers of criticism when he compiled his *Collected Works*.

BITTER BIERCE

James Mortimer: *Figaro*, *The Cuckoo*, *The Bat*, etc. They were all short-lived, and the files have not been preserved. Mortimer is, however, an important figure in Bierce's London days for he was the man who got Bierce the job of defending the Empress Eugénie. During the whole course of the Second Empire no journalist was more persistent in criticizing the royal family than Henri de Rochefort. In *The Second Empire* Philip Guedalla described him thus: "There was a surge of journalism when the restrictions came off, and anxious gentlemen sat at the Ministry of Interior scanning the new publications for signs of *lèse-majesté*. Their quest was amply satisfied in the summer of 1868 when M. Rochefort, who had made something of a reputation for seditious innuendo in the newspapers, brought out a paper in a bright red cover and called it *La Lanterne*. He was a remarkable young man with black hair and a piercing eye; his gifts combined a rare genius for burlesque with that verbal felicity which can maintain a steady flow of witticisms; and he had not yet discovered his total incapacity for living contentedly under any form of government whatever. The bland impertinence of his first number, of which he hoped to sell four thousand copies, brought him a circulation of one hundred thousand, and his malice set Paris tittering every Saturday. The note was struck in his opening sentence— '*La France contient, dit l'*Almanach impérial, *trente-six millions de sujets, sans compter les sujets de mécontentment'* —and he ran easily through every tone of derision from irony to abuse. The ways of ministers, the Empress and her crinolines, the Emperor and his dog made weekly appearance in his sardonic *revue;* the accomplishments of Queen Hortense and the paternity of her son, the dialectic of M. Rouher, the antics of the police, the stale flavour of old scandals about Mexico, and the whole under-side of the Imperial scene were M. Rochefort's stock-in-trade."[13] Rochefort was eventually exiled to

[13]Philip Guedalla, *The Second Empire*, pp. 388–389.

New Caledonia, and it was his escape from
there and return to Europe that aroused anew
the fear of his pen in the breast of Empress
Eugénie. It was understood that he did not
intend to let his animus die with the Empire
but would persecute her even in her English
exile, so she cast about for ways and means of
circumventing him. Her advisers had the
bright idea of copywriting his favourite title,
La Lanterne, and issuing a few copies of a
journal under that name. They accurately
assumed that if he had to publish his journal
with a new name it would be extremely difficult for him to reach his public. They were
willing to go to any expense to circumvent
him. It was this sheet, called *The Lantern*,
that Bierce was given to handle. Rochefort
gave up the struggle—if he had intended to
struggle—without a blow. Bierce enjoyed the
episode exceedingly and summed it up with
considerable gusto: "On the 18th of May,
1874, there was published at the corner of St.
Bride Street and Shoe Lane, E. C., London,

the first number of '*The Lantern*—Appearing
Occasionally. Illuminated by Faustine. Price,
sixpence.' It was a twelve-page paper (the text
written by Bierce alone) with four pages of
superb illustrations in six colours. I winced
when I contemplated its artistic and mechanical excellence, for I knew at what a price that
quality had been obtained. A gold mine would
be required to maintain that journal, and that
journal could by no means ever be itself a gold
mine. A copy lies before me as I write and
noting it critically I cannot keep from thinking
that the illuminated title-page of this pioneer
in the field of chromatic journalism is the
finest thing of the kind that ever came from a
press. . . .

"By way (as I supposed) of gratitude for
the use of the title of his defunct journal it had
been suggested by Mr. Mortimer that he
(Rochefort) be given a little wholesome ad-
monition here and there in the paper and I
cheerfully complied. M. Rochefort had escaped
from New Caledonia some months before. A

disagreeable cartoon was devised for his discomfort and he received a number of such delicate attentions as that following, which in the issue of July 15th greeted him on his arrival in England along with his distinguished compatriot, M. Pascal Grousset.

"'M. Rochefort is a gentleman who has lost his standing. There have been greater falls than his. Kings before now have become servitors, honest men bandits, thieves communists. Insignificant in his fortunes as in his abilities, M. Rochefort, who was never very high, is not now very low—he has avoided the falsehood of extremes: never quite a count, he is now but half a convict. Having missed eminence that would have given him culmination, he is also denied the obscurity that would bring him misconstruction. He is not even a *misérable;* he is a person. It is curious to note how persistently this man has perverted his gifts. With talents that might have corrupted panegyric, he preferred to refine detraction; fitted to disgrace the *salon,* he has elected to adorn the cell; the qualities that would have endeared him to a blackguard he has wasted upon Pascal Grousset.

"'As we write, it is reported that this person is in England. It is further affirmed that it is his intention to proceed to Belgium or Switzerland to fight certain journalists who have not had the courtesy to suppress the truth about him, though he never told it of them. We presume, however, this rumor is false; M. Rochefort must retain enough of the knowledge he acquired when he was esteemed a gentleman to be aware that a meeting between him and a journalist is now impossible. This is the more to be regretted, because M. Paul de Cassagnac would have much pleasure in taking M. Rochefort's life and we in lamenting his fall.

"'M. Rochefort, we believe, is already suffering from an unhealed wound. It is his mouth.'

"There was a good deal of such 'scurril jesting' in the paper, especially in a department called 'Prattle' [a name Bierce was to make famous later]. There were verses on all manner of subjects—mostly the nobility and their works and ways, from the viewpoint of disapproval—and epigrams, generally ill-humorous, like the following, headed *Novum Organum:*

> In Bacon see the culminating prime
> Of British intellect and British crime.
> He died, and Nature, settling his affairs,
> Parted his powers among us, his heirs:
> To each a pinch of common-sense, for seed,
> And, to develop it, a pinch of greed.
> Each frugal heir, to make the gift suffice,
> Buries the talent to manure the vice.

"When the first issue of *The Lantern* appeared I wrote Mr. Mortimer, . . . urging him . . . to alter the character of the journal. He replied that it suited him as it was and he would let me know when to prepare 'copy' for the second number. That eventually appeared on July 15th. I never was instructed to prepare any more copy, and there has been, I believe, no further issue of that interesting sheet as yet. . . .

"Being in London later in the year, I received through Mortimer an invitation to visit the poor lady [the Empress], *en famille*, at Chiselhurst; but the iron rules of imperial etiquette, even in exile, required that the hospitable request be made in the form of a 'command,' my republican independence took alarm and I had the incivility to disobey; and I still think it a sufficient distinction to be probably the only American journalist who was ever employed by an Empress in so congenial a pursuit as the pursuit of another journalist."[14]

In London Bierce learned his trade as a writing man, and the ideals he acquired there stuck by him more or less all his life. It is worth pointing out again that he had a high and adulatory notion of the English. He used his notion as a rod with which to beat the American dog. Yet it must be admitted that the influences to which he was subjected in London were not of the highest. The figures

[14]Cf. "Bits of Autobiography," in *Collected Works*, Vol. I. Quotation made with the permission of A. & C. Boni, Inc.

with whom he associated were not (with one or two exceptions whom he himself does not mention), and never became, anything more than competent journalists. In London, as elsewhere throughout his career, Bierce rarely associated with men of his own stature. Consequently he suffered from lack of criticism. Naturally doing much better work than any of his associates, he never felt the spur to do work of a quality that his full powers could easily encompass. From his own reminiscences of the period he was also, so it seems, considerably taken in by the Bohemian atmosphere in which he moved. There is more than a bit of braggadocio in his statement: "We worked too hard, dined too well, frequented too many clubs and went to bed too late in the forenoon. In short, we diligently, conscientiously and with a perverse satisfaction burned the candle of life at both ends and in the middle." There is a good deal of truth in the comment of a writer in the London *Athenæum* (1909): "Mr. Bierce seems to have taken very seriously the somewhat raffish celebrities of Fleet Street to the honour of whose acquaintance and orgies he was admitted; and would have us think that not Jamshyd himself gloried and drank as he and they. As a fact, we do not believe that they did his morals any material harm, but we suspect that they influenced his literary standards for life, and that, conscious of it or no, his aim ever since has been to write what any one of these judges would have declared to be 'damned good stuff.'"[15]

Whatever London may have meant to him it did not mean enough to keep him there, for in 1876 he was once more in San Francisco, where he was to remain for twenty years, save for one brief sojourn in the Black Hills of Dakota. Back in his old haunts Bierce clearly had the advantage over the other journalists of the city. He had, if nothing else, the prestige of English journalistic experience. He quickly

---

[15]Some time during this London period Bierce made a trip to Paris, but no record of it survives other than a casual reference in one of his letters to having seen the gargoyles on Notre Dame.

asserted his claims to preëminence and entered upon the period in which he was the literary dictator of the West. His word was law.

He was thirty-four years old and a man of striking appearance. He changed very little as he grew older. He was close on to six feet tall, of military bearing, and of such extraordinary vitality that young ladies asserted that they could feel him ten feet away. His hair was curly and blond, and so was his moustache. His eyes are subject for remark by writers who do not particularly describe him otherwise. They were blue, remarkably piercing, and were overhung with shaggy blond eyebrows. His expression was one of intelligence and vigour. He was altogether a man of mark.

In personal habits he was no less out of the ordinary. He made a fetish of his personal appearance and spent an unusual amount of time and care over his toilet. His nephew, Carlton, asserted, perhaps in ridicule, that Bierce shaved all over every day. He had a modesty of a pathological sort. It was his boast that no woman, not even his wife, had seen him entirely naked. He even extended his modesty to others and once threatened in all seriousness to shoot George Sterling if he persisted in his innocent intention of appearing before Bierce's niece in a swimming costume that deviated but slightly from the normal.

He was extremely fond of bicycle riding and indulged frequently in the sport. He was also an expert canoeist from boyhood and in his early Washington days took up the sport again with zest after neglecting it for years. For many years he kept lizards as pets, and one in particular became so friendly as to sit on his shoulder while he wrote. He was, said Bierce, his best and most severe critic. Later, in Washington, he kept a canary, and Mr. E. D. Coblentz writes:[16] "My acquaintance with Bierce was slight. I met him in 1900 in Washington, D. C. I was a boy at that time, and recall going with him to Mt. Vernon; and there he picked up a small mud turtle and asked me

[16]In a letter to me dated June 29, 1928.

to carry it in my camera case for him. He explained to me that he had had a horned toad which had lived with him for two years. He insisted that the toad had intelligence, that he always placed it on the table when he dined alone, and allowed the little beast the freedom of his bed. He wanted the mud turtle to take the place of the toad." To these pets, and indeed to all dumb animals except dogs, Bierce was generous and kind. Dogs he could not endure. Once he received a snapshot of a friend in which a dog appeared. In thanking him for it he announced that he would blot out the dog before putting the picture on the mantelpiece.

Bierce liked his liquor and prided himself on being an "eminent tankard man." His favourite drink was wine, but when out with companions he drank whatever his companions chose. He matched drink for drink and inevitably ordered the last drink for himself. Those who tried to drink him out of the picture always regretted it. George Sterling could recall having seen Bierce drunk on but one occasion and that when he was seventy years old, and his drinking companion was Jack London! Bierce was also something of a gourmet and could wax eloquent on the low state of American cooking.

Quite early in this second period in San Francisco he acquired the disease that made life a burden for him the rest of his days. One evening he went for a walk in a cemetery and to rest lay down on a tombstone. He fell asleep, and while asleep a fog came up. When he awoke he was thoroughly chilled and thereafter suffered from asthma. This disease prevented him from living in the city of San Francisco and compelled him to spend his time at various little towns in the hills around about from whence he sent his copy. He found the climate of the East, in later days, more suitable for him and the Eastern winter most satisfactory of all, from which fact he deduced that there was an Eskimo in his family line.

When he first returned from London Bierce contributed to the *Wasp* with regularity and to the *Argonaut*.[17] Barring occasional contributions elsewhere these two papers seem to have been his principal source of income until William Randolph Hearst hired him for the *Examiner* in 1881. It was in the *Wasp* and *Argonaut* days that he was able to make his personal influence felt most strongly. In the *Examiner* days he was chiefly in the country and exerted his influence through the printed word almost exclusively.

It is difficult to understand at this distance the extraordinary dictatorship that Bierce built up. San Francisco was a more isolated city then than it is now, and naturally the local gods had more power. It is revealing, perhaps, to collect the terms used by those recalling Bierce of those days: The Great Cham, Johnson the Second, more powerful than Ben of

---

[17]Cf. the *Argonaut*, June 9, 1928: "... there is an error in chronology into which George Sterling and most of the other biographers of Bierce fell. Sterling wrote that before going to London in 1872 Bierce held 'editorial positions consecutively on several San Francisco weeklies, the *News-Letter*, the *Argonaut*, and the *Wasp*.' As a fact, Bierce's connection with the *Argonaut* began in 1877, a year after his return from London."

the Mermaid, the Radamanthus of Letters. Joseph Lewis French, who knew Bierce in those days, has written as clear an exposition of Bierce's position as anyone:[18] "No man's reputation as a writer was quite made in those days until Bierce had pronounced on him. We were his slaves and obedient to his will, and right royally he cracked the whip over us. He even went so far as to pass judgment on the private affairs of the devotees of his circle which finally led to estrangements. . . . His disciples gradually fell away as the message became more insistent. That was the fault of Bierce; he did not know when to stop and soothe with humanity the wounds his biting sarcasm made." No one felt quite safe in his own opinion, and Bierce's ratification was necessary before any of his disciples trusted their own judgments. This is neatly illustrated by Bob Davis's anecdote apropos Stephen Crane's *Red Badge of Courage*. ". . . I found time to read *The Red Badge of Courage*, with

[18]In *Pearson's Magazine*, Vols. XXXVIII and XXXIX, 1913.

which I became reasonably familiar. My written report to Mr. Doxey [a San Francisco bookseller] stated in substance that *The Red Badge of Courage* was a courageous performance that thrilled with the recital of life and death because the author had 'immortalized bravery without being called upon to exhibit it,' or words to that effect. . . . The following week I met Ambrose Bierce and William C. Morrow, two distinguished men of letters who have since joined the shades, and spoke to them of *The Red Badge*. Both had read it. I do not recall Morrow's exact criticism except that it was reasonably laudatory. Bierce's observation remains with me: 'This young man,' said he, 'has the power to feel. He knows nothing of war, yet he is drenched in blood. Most beginners who deal with this subject spatter themselves merely with ink.' . . . This, coming from the brilliant critic who wrote that classic single-line review, 'The covers of this book are too far apart,' encouraged me in the belief that I had at least interpreted the fourteenth

45

child of Jonathan Townley Crane, D. D.''[19]

Bierce's literary influence was narrowing and hardening. His great contribution to his disciples was a worship of clarity in thought and expression. But it seems quite correct to say that he was not the sort of man to exercise determining power over beginning writers. His sympathies were not wide enough. He found it difficult to tolerate anything that diverged far from his own narrow standards of excellence. He acquired greater tolerance when he grew older. His ability to take his dictatorship seriously was greatly assisted by the fact that he had an absolute, and consequently unwholesome, belief in his own powers of discerning the right. What he thought was right, and any dissent from his position was not only heresy but treason. If an erstwhile disciple became so wilful as to assert his independence he was showered with horrid invective and shoved down to the lower rings of hell.

---

[19]Robert H. Davis: Introduction to "Tales of Two Wars" in *The Works of Stephen Crane.*

BITTER BIERCE

It has been remarked that he had very little contact with writers of anything approaching his own stature. That he held aloof from the literary rabble is not so astonishing after all. He was easily offended by low literary ideals. But more usually he found himself unable to get along with writers other than those pursuing his own or a similar course. He knew Edwin Markham, but broke with him over "The Man with the Hoe" of which he violently disapproved. Yet he continued to admire Markham's benignity of character. He admired Jack London's potentialities but detested his social philosophy and concessions to the popular taboo relating to sex. His personal encounter with London is illuminating. In 1912 Bierce attended the San Francisco Bohemian Club's High Jinks in the company of George Sterling. Sterling tells the story: ". . . After a few hours in camp he inquired as to the whereabouts of London, whom he knew to be attending the Jinks. 'Oh, you mustn't meet him,' I replied. 'You'd be at each other's throats in five minutes.' 'Nonsense!' exclaimed Bierce, drawing his blond, shaggy brows together. 'Bring him on. I'll treat him like a Dutch uncle.' So I disentangled London from the poker-game to which he gave his forenoons, and presented him. The two men conversed in the friendliest manner though signs of an armed peace were not lacking to my anxious eye. However, they were never to cross swords in argument, and the midnight of the grove-play saw us accompanying Bierce to his brother's home, to reach which we had to cross the river in a row boat and then walk over a mile along the railroad track. We managed the river despite the ocean of our potations, and London and I were ambling rather unsteadily along the ties when he suddenly said: 'Why, where the hell's Ambrose?' Sure enough, Bierce had vanished. We retraced the rough way along the track, calling loudly, and were soon rewarded by the sound of his voice from the bottom of the twenty-foot embankment at our right. He had stumbled, lost his arm-clasp on London's shoulder, and slid head-first down the steep bank, to a fern bed where he seemed content to lie. We descended and helped him to his feet. He was not even scratched, and we proceeded to our destination, where he and London sat up the rest of the night, consuming a bottle each of Three Star Martel. God knows of what they talked! I was to awaken at seven with the worst headache of my life. Truly they were made of the stuff of heroes."[20] Yet Bierce never ceased to execrate London's socialism. Bierce, whose final comment was always, "Nothing matters," could never come very close to a man like London, to whom everything mattered tremendously.

Bierce also knew Joaquin Miller, but slightly. Similarly his acquaintance with Mark Twain was of no particular significance: "No, I never had any row (nor much acquaintance) with Mark Twain—met him but two or three times." The two men of whom he thought most in his latter days, George Sterling and Herman

[20]Sterling, in the *American Mercury*, October, 1925.

49

Scheffauer, were his protégés, particularly the former. They were much younger and not in any way his equals. Samuel Loveman, who has published the correspondence he had with him, stood in the same relationship. Most of those who are alleged to have been his intimates—H. L. Mencken, Arthur Brisbane, Will Irwin—all turn out on investigation to have known him but slightly.

In truth, Bierce's only literary intimate of somewhat equal stature was Percival Pollard. Just when Bierce met Pollard is not clear, but it must have been after 1896, when Bierce had established himself in Washington. Once established the acquaintance flourished. Bierce always contrived to meet Pollard whenever he visited New York. He was immoderately fond of New York and visited it as frequently as he could. He always stayed at the old Hotel Navarre, Seventh Avenue and Thirty-eighth Street. He found New York to be a great place for "owling, dining, and booze." On February 29, 1904, he wrote to George Sterling of Pollard: "I passed yesterday with Percival Pollard, viewing the burnt district of Baltimore. He's a queer duck whom I like, and he likes your work. I'm sending you a copy of 'The Papyrus' with his 'rehabilitation' of the odious Oscar Wilde. Wilde's work is all right, but what can one do with the work of one whose name one cannot speak before women?" In 1905 he spent the month of July with Pollard at Saybrook, Connecticut. In the winter of 1907 the two made a tour of the Civil War battlefields together, going as far South as Galveston, Texas, and returning home via Key West and Florida. If Bierce thought highly of Pollard, the latter returned the compliment with interest in *Their Day in Court*. Pollard's funeral brought Bierce and H. L. Mencken together in the same carriage, and Mencken found Bierce to be the most thoroughgoing cynic he had ever met.

Bierce's disavowal of any quarrel with Twain points to an almost indispensable part of his friendships: he usually quarrelled sooner or later. He eventually quarrelled with Sterling, but Sterling magnanimously destroyed the scurrilous letters that marked the end of their long friendship.[21] However, Sterling never allowed it to interfere with his opinion of Bierce the writer and devoted some of his last efforts before his suicide to advancing Bierce's reputation.[22]

Bierce's relations with women were not a whit more successful. In one of his letters he remarks: "Girls is pizen but not necessarily fatal. I've taken 'em in large doses all my life, and suffered pangs enough to equip a number of small Hells, but never has one of them paralyzed the inner working man." As already

[21]The causes of the quarrel were three: (1) Sterling's socialism; (2) Sterling's alleged misrepresentation of how one of Bierce's books was financed (this accusation Sterling says was based on a delusion on Bierce's part); (3) Sterling's alleged gossip campaign against Bierce's relations with women. (Cf. below on Bierce's engagement of 1910.) This last Sterling has also refuted. The whole episode proves the truth of Albert's analysis of Bierce's mental habits with regard to slights, real and imagined.

[22]Cf. especially the Preface to The Modern Library edition of Bierce's *In the Midst of Life*. According to the publisher's note: "Two weeks before his tragic death, George Sterling, lifelong friend of Ambrose Bierce, completed his introduction. . . . It was the last writing from his pen."

noted his married life was a conspicuous failure, and though it contributed to his bitterness about women it did not deter him from seeking their company. His relations with them were conditioned, too, by a consistent antifeminism. Nevertheless, he found passing happiness in their company. Some of his best letters are addressed to women, and to them—and to dumb animals—he showed his most kindly side. Writing of the summer of 1889, Mrs. J. C. McCrackin, for whose book of short stories, *The Woman Who Lost Him*, Bierce wrote an introduction, and who was to receive some of the last letters he wrote before going to Mexico, says: "A very pleasant summer was that of 1889, though it went out with a pall of smoke hanging over it. Ambrose Bierce came up in the Santa Cruz mountains early in the year, with the avowed intention of remaining through the season. Ambrose Bierce, the best-hated and best-loved man in California, whose renown followed wherever the fear his name scattered has penetrated

first. Yet he could be so good and kind and
companionable. Though he could have been
Mr. McCrackin's son in years, he chose to act
as if they were old cronies together, greatly
to Mac's delight, for Bierce, too, claimed to be
countrybred, and he would turn to Mac for
corroboration when he said, 'We used to do so
on the farm, didn't we, Mac?' But he could be
merciless in his sarcasm; he hated hypocrisy and
was utterly without fear." The fire which swept
the mountain did not burn down the house in
which Bierce was staying. The McCrackins, however, lost everything. When Bierce and the Mc-
Crackins went to view the ruins: "Mr. Bierce,
always sympathetic, had thrown his cape, a
remnant of his soldier-days, around me, for my
clothes were in tatters. . . . In every way did
this much maligned man show his sympathy."[23]

In 1910 Bierce became engaged to marry a
charming middle-aged California woman, but
this was made impossible by idle scandal-

[23]These reminiscences of Bierce are included in "The Romantic
History of Josephine Clifford McCrackin," by George Wharton
James, prefaced to *The Woman Who Lost Him.*

mongering about his relations to some idolizing women of Sag Harbor, Long Island, where he spent a few weeks of the summer of 1911. (Cf. Ft. 21 pt. 3.) Looking back over this phase of Bierce's life George Sterling wrote: ". . . Bierce found his main happiness, intermittent as that may have been, in the society of the woman for whom he cared most at the time." Incidentally his favourite toast was: "Here's to woman! Would that we could fall into her arms without falling into her hands."[24]

In 1880 there occurred one of the most obscure episodes in Bierce's life. He left San Francisco and went to the Black Hills of South Dakota to become manager of a gold mine. What induced him to undertake this venture, how long it lasted, and why he gave it up to return to San Francisco I do not know. The

[24]It is a curious commentary on this phase of Bierce's career that he anticipated a dogma of modern psychology when he wrote in "The Death of Halpin Frayser": "In these two romantic natures was manifest in a signal way that neglected phenomenon, *the dominance of the sexual element in all the relations of life*, strengthening, softening, and beautifying even those of consanguinity." [Italics inserted.]

only precise bit of information about the
whole transaction is contained in an unimportant "bit of autobiography" which recounts
his adventure with highwaymen when he was
carrying $30,000 to the bank, guarded, effi-
ciently it proved, by Boone May, an ex-thief
and notorious murderer.

When William Randolph Hearst was building up his first newspaper, the San Francisco
Examiner, in the early 'eighties, he asked
Bierce to contribute a feature article to the Sunday issue. This became known as "Prattle, a
Transient Record of Individual Opinion." It ran
from 1881 until 1896, until Bierce was moved to
Washington. "Prattle" extended Bierce's fame
and influence enormously. He did not visit the
office of the *Examiner* at all frequently, but
lived in the hills and sent his copy in by mail.
He customarily wrote it in longhand. He wrote
easily and always at the last possible moment.

"Prattle" was one of the earliest columns
and is now easily one of the most famous.

BITTER BIERCE

Unlike Eugene Field's or B. L. T.'s, Bierce's
column is not famous as the source of charming wit and *vers de société*, but as the source of
some of the most scorching wit, irony, satire,
and bludgeoning that have ever been printed
by an American newspaper. Into "Prattle"
Bierce poured his scorn of the world. To-day
we are more used to severe and forthright criticism, but in Bierce's time, as everyone knows,
the more usual course was silence. Into this
atmosphere Bierce projected himself. He hit
out without fear and without compromise.
The wonder of it is that he was rarely answered
back and never as effectively as he had hit in
the first place. When, on one occasion, he hit
a rival writer a bit harder than usual, he received warning that he would be shot on sight.
In reply he announced that he would leave a
designated building at a specified time, proceed down a specified side of the street and
enter a second building. His enemy was in-
vited to take the occasion offered to shoot at
him. He carried out his end of the bargain,

but the offended one left town. Bierce was well known to be a dead shot.

Bierce's especial prey was fools, frauds, crooks of business and politics, and in general those who deviated from his own high standards of what was right and honourable. He always aimed to annihilate his victim at a blow. He was never tediously polite. Neither did he believe in being vague. It was part of his procedure to make it plain to the weakest intelligence who was attacked. It seemed to him that half the point was lost if anyone failed to see at a glance who was meant. Since he was writing for a local audience a good many of the individual figures attacked are unknown or of small interest to-day. Bierce himself had no illusions about the national, let alone cosmic, importance of his victims, but he proceeded on the assumption that principles are always violated by individuals —mostly by unimportant individuals in the larger view of things—but that if principles are to be supported it is necessary to swat every violator of them without regard to their individual importance. He held that the low state of public morals is not due to our low ideals but to our tolerance of specific violators of them. As he put it: "I care nothing for principles—they are lumber and rubbish. What concerns our happiness and welfare, as affectable by our fellow men, is conduct. 'Principles, not men,' is a rogue's cry; rascality's counsel to stupidity, the noise of the duper duping on his dupe. He shouts it most loudly and with the keenest sense of its advantage who most desires inattention to his own conduct, or to that forecast of it, his character. As to sin, that has an abundance of expounders and is already universally known to be wicked. What more can be said against it, and why go on repeating that? The thing is a trifle word worn, whereas the sinner cometh up as a flower every day, fresh, ingenuous, and inviting. Sin is not at all dangerous to society; what does all the mischief is the sinner. Crime has no arms to thrust into the public treasury and the private; no hands with which to cut a throat; no tongue to wreck a reputation withal. I would no more attack it than I would attack an isosceles triangle, or Hume's 'phantasm floating in a void.' My chosen enemy must be something that has a skin for my switch, a head for my cudgel—something that can smart and ache. I have no quarrel with abstractions; so far as I know they are all good citizens."[25] But just because his attacks were specific they earned him a reputation of a dual nature. By some he was naturally idolized as a great wit and enemy of corruption without equal and to others he was a "poor professional polecat" and, in the words of Franklin K. Lane, "A hideous monster, so like a mixture of dragon, lizard, bird, and snake as to be unnameable."

In addition to his war on the unrighteous, Bierce used "Prattle" as a vehicle for the propagation of his heretical notions about capital punishment, prison discipline, dogs,

[25]Cf. *Collected Works*, Vol. XI, pp. 197–198.

charity, the industrial problem, war, politics, emancipated women, literature, and a hundred other things. But like all columns of this general kind, "Prattle" was more lustrous when it first appeared than the parts of it that have been reprinted now appear. There is no doubt at all that Bierce enjoyed writing it, but when he looked back on it in perspective he had some doubts about the wisdom of doing anything to revive the material buried in it. He wrote George Sterling in 1903: "You make me shudder when you say you are reading the 'Prattle' of years. I haven't it and should hardly dare to read it if I had. There is so much in it to deplore—so much that is not wise—so much that was the expression of a mood or a whim—so much that was not altogether sincere—so many half truths, and so forth. Make allowances, I beg, and where you cannot, just forgive."

Riding high on the success of "Prattle" and in full possession of his powers, Bierce during the 'nineties produced his most important contributions to literature. In 1891 appeared *Tales of Soldiers and Civilians* (now known as *In the Midst of Life*). To-day Bierce's reputation largely rests on his short stories. In his own day he was better known as a journalist. He could not get a single story of his printed in a national magazine. Not only did the magazines reject his stories with consistent unanimity, but the publishing houses turned down his first volume and he was finally forced to let it be issued by a business friend, Mr. E. L. G. Steele, with the now-famous preface: "Denied existence by the chief publishing houses of the country, this book owes itself to Mr. E. L. G. Steele, merchant, of this city. In attesting Mr. Steele's faith in his judgment and his friend, it will serve its author's main and best ambition." The next year he issued a book through F. J. Schulte of Chicago which is still the subject of controversy. Conventionally it is attributed to Bierce with a vague reservation that he derived the bulk of the story from a roughly translated version of a

German story. *The Monk and the Hangman's Daughter* is entirely unlike anything else that Bierce wrote. It is an idyll. As a study of religious life it stands high in American fiction which is none too well supplied with fictional treatments of religious subjects outside of Sunday-school books. In the preface to the original edition it is stated: "The foundation of this narrative is an old manuscript originally belonging to the Franciscan monastery at Berchtesgaden, Bavaria. The manuscript was obtained from a peasant by Herr Richard Voss, of Heidelberg, from whose German version this is an adaptation. D. and B." Subsequently Dr. Danziger mastered English and published books of his own, on the title page of one of which he laid claim to being the author of *The Monk*. This assertion aroused Bierce's anger, for not only did it place him in an ambiguous position, but it took away the credit Dr. Danziger himself had agreed belonged to Herr Voss. Consequently, when *The Monk* was reissued Bierce wrote a new preface, which read in part as follows: "Many years ago—probably in 1890—Dr. Gustav Adolf Danziger brought to me in San Francisco what he said was a translation by himself of a German story by that brilliant writer, Herr Richard Voss, of Heidelberg. As Dr. Danziger had at that time a most imperfect acquaintance with the English language, he asked me to rewrite his version of Herr Voss's work for publication in this country. In reading it I was struck by what seemed to me certain possibilities of amplification, and I agreed to do the work if given a free hand by both author and translator. To this somewhat ill-considered proposal, which I supposed would make an end of the matter, I was afterward assured that the author, personally known to the translator, had assented. The result was this book, published by F. J. Schulte & Company of Chicago. Almost coincidentally in point of time the publishers failed, and it was, so far as I know, never put upon the market. [It was.—C. H. G.] Never having seen the original story, and having no skill in German anyhow, I am unable to say what liberties Dr. Danziger may have taken with his author's text; to me he professed to have taken none; yet, in recent books of his he is described on the title pages as 'Author of *The Monk and the Hangman's Daughter*—a statement that seems to justify, if not compel, this brief account of a matter which, though not particularly important, has given rise to more discussion than I have cared to engage in. By a merely literary artifice the author of the German tale professed to have derived it from another writing, and in the Schulte version appeared the note following [quoted above]: . . . I have always felt that this was inadequate acknowledgment of the work of Herr Voss, for whom I have the profoundest admiration. Not the least part of my motive and satisfaction in republishing lies in the opportunity that it supplies for doing justice to one to whose splendid imagination the chief credit of the tale is due. My light opinion of the credit due to anyone else is attested by my retention of Dr. Danziger's name on the title page. In this version the work that came into my hands from his has been greatly altered and extended. *Ambrose Bierce*, Washington, D. C., November 29, 1906." Recently Dr. Danziger, now using the name of Adolphe de Castro, has published notice that he has the right to insist that his name be included on the title page of all future editions of the story as co-author. It is not at all clear just what credit Mr. Danziger now assigns to Herr Voss. As a sidelight on the whole episode it may be remarked that it seems that while Bierce was very friendly with Danziger in the early 'nineties he later had a violent disagreement with him, so violent indeed that he broke a substantial cane over the doctor's head. Bierce had the cane repaired with silver bands and preserved it carefully. He frequently showed the cane to friends and explained how it was broken, with gusto.

In 1893 *Can Such Things Be?* appeared in

New York City. And it was followed in succession by *Black Beetles in Amber* (San Francisco, 1895), *Fantastic Fables* (New York, 1899), *Shapes of Clay* (San Francisco, 1903), *The Cynic's Word Book* (New York, 1906), *Write It Right* (New York, 1909), and *The Shadow on the Dial and Other Essays* (San Francisco, 1909). Between 1909 and 1912 most of these books were included in a collected edition. This edition, much to Bierce's disgust, was only printed in two hundred and fifty sets. It was issued by the Neale Publishing Company of Washington and New York. Of all these books only one, *The Cynic's Word Book* (now *The Devil's Dictionary*), was issued by a regular publishing house. As a rule friends undertook to issue the books to the accompaniment of dire prophecies of failure from Bierce. He had no faith whatsoever in the reading public. "My work," he wrote, "sells tremendously in Mr. Hearst's newspapers, at the price of a small fraction of one cent.Offered by itself, in one-dollar and two-dollar lots, it tempts nobody to fall over his own feet in the rush to buy."

In 1896 Bierce went to Washington to fight a measure Collis P. Huntington was trying to get through Congress. Under his agreements with the government relative to his railroads, Huntington was liable for the payment of $75,000,000, and he was seeking to be relieved of the obligation. Hearst, among others, was opposed to his move, which failed, and sent Bierce to Washington to follow the game. Bierce held Huntington to be the "meanest man who ever lived."[26] (Joaquin Miller, on the other hand, dedicated his collected works to Huntington!) When Bierce arrived in Washington, Huntington heard of it and cynically asked: "How much does he want?" Such cynicism about his motives made Bierce furiously angry, and he replied: "Please go back

[26]Bierce's epitaph on Huntington was:
> Here Huntington's ashes long have lain
> Whose loss is our own eternal gain,
> For while he exercised all his powers
> Whatever he gained, the loss was ours.
> —*The Devil's Dictionary*, p. 202.

and tell him that my price is about seventy-five million dollars. If, when he is ready to pay, I happen to be out of town, he may hand it to my friend, the Treasurer of the United States."

After the battle was over and Huntington defeated, Bierce remained in Washington and was attached to the Washington Bureau of the New York *American*. His stuff was first printed in the New York paper and then syndicated. It gave him the largest audience he ever had, but since the editorial hand lay heavy on him he didn't enjoy the experience and wrote little that he didn't consider twaddle. In addition he for a short while conducted a department in the *Cosmopolitan* entitled "The Passing Show." This also he considered to be of no importance. In fact, his last years as a newspaper man were most unsatisfactory. He complained bitterly about his fate, hated most of the stuff he wrote and the papers he wrote for. About the only thing in which he took any satisfaction was the check he got each week. "My stuff in the New York

American . . . is mere piffle, written without
effort, purpose or care. My department in the
Cosmopolitan is a failure, as I told Millard it
would be. . . . The venture and title were
Hearst's notion, but the title so handicaps me
than I can do nothing right. I shall drop it."
(February 3, 1906.)

There has been a good deal of speculation
about his relations with William Randolph
Hearst. Bierce's personal attitude seems to
have been a cross between admiration and distaste. He admired Hearst's astonishing, con-
quering arrogance and detested his yellow
journalism. He resigned from his position
several times before he finally concluded his
journalistic career in 1909, but was always
coaxed back. Yet he did not scruple to speak
of Hearst in the same breath as Johan Most,
and in his essay, "A Mad World," in which
he imagined that it was impossible that so
gorgeous a spectacle as the world could be
anything other than a figment of his disor-
dered imagination he wrote: "But the mental

feat in which I take most satisfaction, and
which I doubt not is most diverting to my
keepers, is that of creating Mr. W. R. Hearst,
pointing his eyes toward the White House
and endowing him with a perilous Jacksonian
ambition to defile it. The Hearst is distinctly
a treasure." And he put his judgment of
Hearst's intellectual attainments into rhyme:

Hearst kept a diary wherein were writ
All that he had of wisdom and of wit.
So the Recording Angel, when Hearst died,
Erased all entries of his own and cried:
"I'll judge you by your diary." Said Hearst:
"Thank you; 'twill show you I am Saint the First."
Straightway producing, jubilant and proud,
That record from a pocket in his shroud.
The Angel slowly turned the pages o'er,
Each stupid line of which he knew before,
Glooming and gleaming as by turns he hit
On shallow sentiment and stolen wit;
Then gravely closed the book and gave it back.
"My friend, you've wandered from your proper track:
You'd never be content this side the tomb—
For big ideas Heaven has little room,
And Hell's no latitude for making mirth,"
He said, and kicked the fellow back to earth.[27]

[27] *The Devil's Dictionary*, p. 70.

BITTER BIERCE

In 1909 Bierce gave up newspaper writing altogether and devoted himself, so far as he worked at all, to preparing the collected edition of his works, which appeared at intervals between 1909 and 1912. This enterprise absorbed most of his energies during these years and gave him little satisfaction. In spite of the work Bierce put into this final edition it is not a monument to his powers. He was too lenient in judging his own work and included much that has no permanent value. It is a discouraging job to read the whole edition, for one has to go over page after page of material in the hope of finding a bright gleam of wit or sense. The edition is obviously the work of an old man fondly cherishing the products of his brilliant youth. But Bierce, of course, did not find his disappointment in the quality of the material he had to deal with. He was disappointed, in the first place, when the edition was limited to two hundred and fifty sets. And he was disappointed in the second place, and yet in a way happy because it proved something discreditable to the human race, at the reluctance of his friends to subscribe to the edition. He wrote to George Sterling: "The man who expects anything more than lip-service from his friends is a very young man. . . . Friends be damned—strangers are the chaps for me." He was relieved when he finally got the proofs of the last volume corrected and could consider the matter closed.

In these years, too, dissatisfaction and discontent ate at his mind. He felt that he was played out. With nothing more to say and with his creative powers gone, he found life a burden. Though his health was as good as could be expected, and although he occasionally came upon new experiences and pleasures —particularly on his trips to California in 1910 and 1912—he could not throw off his depression. No doubt he was seeking an escape from it when he made his abortive gesture toward marriage in 1910. And anyway a crucial blow to his continued zest for life was the death of his son Leigh in 1901. A year

later he wrote: "Leigh died a year ago. I wish
I could stop counting the days."

In the fall of 1913 his dissatisfaction came
to a climax, and he planned a trip to Mexico
and perhaps to South America. That he regarded it as the final phase of his life that
would in all probability end in death there is
little doubt. That he planned it as a melo-
dramatic disappearance and suicide there is
every doubt in the world. He simply preferred,
if he must face death, to face it in action.
Shortly before he went away he visited friends
in New Jersey and announced his intention.
"'When you come back,' I said, 'come first to
us and rest.' He did not answer; but after a
little he said softly, 'When I come back . . .'
and I saw him turn his face quite quickly
away."[28] But whatever his motive he carefully put his affairs in order, let his friends
know of his plans, and set out. Typical of the
farewell letters he wrote are those to his old

[28]Cf. "Mr. Boythorn-Bierce," by Ruth Guthrie Harding, the
Bookman (N. Y.), August, 1925.

friend, Mrs. J. C. McCrackin. The book referred to is Mrs. McCrackin's *The Woman Who Lost Him*.

Washington, Sept. 10, 1913.

DEAR JOE:

The reason that I did not answer your letter sooner is —I have been away (in New York) and did not have it with me. I suppose I shall not see your book for a long time, for I am going away and have no notion when I shall return. I expect to go to, perhaps across, South America—possibly via Mexico, if I can get through without being stood up against a wall and shot as a gringo. But that is better than dying in bed, is it not? If Dunc did not need you so badly I'd ask you to get your hat and come along. God bless and keep you.

Washington, Sept. 13, 1913.

DEAR JOE:

Thank you for the book. I thank you for your friendship—and much more besides. This is to say good-by at the end of a pleasant correspondence in which your woman's prerogative of having the last word is denied to you. Before I could receive it I shall be gone. But some time, somewhere, I hope to hear from you again. Yes, I shall go into Mexico with a pretty definite purpose, which, however, is not at present disclosable. You must try to forgive my obstinacy in not "perishing" where I am. I want to be where something worth while is going on, or where nothing whatever is going on.

Most of what is going on in your own country is extremely distasteful to me.

Pray for me? Why, yes, dear—that will not harm either of us. I loathe religions, a Christian gives me qualms and a Catholic sets my teeth on edge, but pray for me just the same, for with all those faults upon your head (it's a nice head, too), I am pretty fond of you, I guess. May you live as long as you want to, and then pass smilingly into the darkness—the good, good darkness.

Devotedly your friend.[29]

But not all of his farewells were so charming. It was at this time that he trampled on his long friendship with George Sterling and wrote the terrible letter to his brother Albert. They, too, were given no chance to reply.

Leaving Washington on October 3, 1913, he first toured the battlefields, reviving his memories of the war years as he had done off and on all during his life. He ended the first lap of his trip in New Orleans and gave an extremely interesting interview to a local paper: "Traveling over the same ground that

[29]Quoted from *Ambrose Bierce*, by Vincent Starrett. W. M. Hill, Chicago, 1920.

he had covered with General Hazen's brigade during the Civil War, Ambrose Bierce, famed writer and noted critic, has arrived in New Orleans. Not that this city was one of the places figuring in his campaigns, for he was here after and not during the war. He has come to New Orleans in a haphazard, fancy-free way, making a trip toward Mexico. The places that he has visited on the way down have become famous in song and story—places where the greatest battles were fought, where the moon shone at night on the burial corps, and where in day the sun shone bright on polished bayonets and the smoke drifted upwards from the cannon mouths. For Mr. Bierce was at Chickamauga; he was at Shiloh, at Murfreesboro, Kenesaw Mountain, Franklin and Nashville. And then when he was wounded during the Atlanta campaign he was invalided home. He 'has never amounted to much since then' he said Saturday. But his stories of the great struggle, living as deathless characterizations of the bloody episodes, stand for what he 'has amounted to since then.' Perhaps it was mourning for the dead over whose battlefields he has been wending his way toward New Orleans that Mr. Bierce was dressed in black. From head to foot he was attired in this color, except where the white cuffs and collar and shirt front showed through. He even carried a walking cane, black as ebony and unrelieved by gold or silver. But his eyes, blue and piercing as when he strove to see through the smoke at Chickamauga, retained all the fire of the indomitable fighter. 'I'm on my way to Mexico, because I like the game,' he said, 'I like fighting; I want to see it. And I don't think Americans are as oppressed there as they say they are, and I want to get at the true facts of the case. Of course, I'm not going into the country if I find it unsafe for Americans to be there, but I want to take a trip diagonally across from northeast to southwest by horseback, and then take ship for South America, go over the Andes and across that continent, if possible, and come back to America again. There is no family that I have to take care of; I've retired from writing and I'm going to take a rest. No, my trip isn't for local color. I've retired just the same as a merchant or business man retires. I'm leaving the field for the younger authors.' An inquisitive question was interjected as to whether Mr. Bierce had acquired a competency only from his writings, but he did not take offence. 'My wants are few, and modest,' he said, 'and my royalties give me quite enough to live on. There isn't much that I need, and I spend my time in quiet travel. For the last five years I haven't done any writing. Don't you think that after a man has worked as long as I have that he deserves a rest? But perhaps after I have rested I might work some more—I can't tell, there are so many things'—and the straightforward blue eyes took on a faraway look, 'there are so many things that might happen between now and when I come back. My trip might take several years, and I'm an old man now."

Except for the thick, snow-white hair no one
would think him old. His hands are steady,
and he stands up straight and tall—perhaps
six feet."[30]

He was next heard from at Chihuahau,
Mexico, from whence he sent his final mes-
sages to his family and friends. The specific
cause of his writing was to acknowledge a
draft that had been forwarded to him there
from Washington by his secretary, Miss Chris-
tianson. After positively proving that he was
in Chihuahua one can give nothing but specu-
lations.

If the number keeps on increasing as many
Mexican towns will claim to have been the
death place of Bierce as Grecian towns claimed
to be the birthplace of Homer. There are
three so far: Sierra Mojada, Icamole, and
Chihuahua. The stories that cluster about
these three towns have a resemblance to each
other, but no one story has yet been authen-

---

[30]Quoted from Miss B. C. Pope's Preface to *The Letters of Ambrose
Bierce* by express permission. Miss Pope says that the item was en-
closed in a letter from Bierce dated November 6, 1913.

ticated. Since September, 1914, when Mrs. H. D. Cowton of Bloomington, Illinois, asked the State Department to try to locate Bierce, it has been impossible to find a trace of him. Both the chargé d'affaires at Mexico City and General Funston failed to achieve anything definite on this first occasion. Fantastic stories about him circulated during the World War, including the story that he had joined the British Army and was doing important work in close association with Lord Kitchener. In 1918 George F. Weeks, a man who had been correspondent in Mexico during the revolutionary disturbances, reported that he had conversed in Mexico City with one Dr. Edmund Melero who claimed that he had been intimately acquainted with Bierce. Melero promised to make inquiries about Bierce's fate. He did so and reported to Weeks that Bierce had deserted to the Constitutionalists from Villa's forces, had later been captured by General Urbina, a Villa leader, near Icamole with an ammunition train. The only other person captured was a Mexican peon. Bierce refused to answer questions and was shot and buried in the village in a shallow grave which he shared with the peon. Dr. Melero later brought a lieutenant of Urbina's to Weeks, who confirmed the story and positively identified Bierce's photograph. George Sterling accepted this story as authentic.[31]

Another version of Bierce's end is that of Dr. Adolphe de Castro Danziger, who was in Mexico from 1922 to 1925. He claims to have talked with Villa in 1923, who was annoyed when Bierce's name was brought up, and to have obtained Villa's own story of Bierce's end—which stopped at a discreet point—and the conclusion of the episode from Villa's close associates. According to this story Bierce was in Chihuahua when Villa captured the town. Bored by the inaction that followed

[31]Cf. Preface to The Modern Library edition of *In the Midst of Life*. Bierce himself shortly before he left for Mexico wrote: "Good-bye— if you hear of my being stood up against a Mexican stone wall and shot to rags please know that I think that a pretty good way to depart this life. It beats old age, disease, or falling down the cellar stairs."

BITTER BIERCE

Bierce got drunk and not only criticized Villa but pointed out the superior virtues of Carranza. For this crime Villa ordered Bierce out of Chihuahua bag and baggage. "*Lo hemos hecho fuera* [We threw him out]," said Villa. It seems, however, that Villa was not content with throwing him out, but also arranged that he be shot down once he got outside the village and his body thrown to the vultures. This was done. This story has been accepted by Robert H. Davis.[32]

The third story is sponsored by one "Tex" O'Reilly, soldier of fortune. He alleges that he discovered Bierce's grave in Sierra Mojada. According to O'Reilly, Bierce met his end at the hands of treacherous Mexican associates. It is unlikely that the matter will ever be

[32]Cf. the New York *Sun*, November 17, 1927. Davis claims to "know a great deal about Bierce, more than most people." However, George Sterling cast very serious doubts on Danziger's reliability—citing particularly the cane episode, noted earlier, as a cause for bias. Cf. Sterling's Introduction to The Modern Library edition of *In the Midst of Life*. Danziger-De Castro repeats the story in the *American Parade*, October, 1926. He also relates other episodes in Bierce's career to justify his title, "Ambrose Bierce as He Really Was." I have used none of the facts that Danziger cites unless they are confirmed from other sources.

finally solved. Bierce's daughter has not yet given up hope, however, for an Associated Press dispatch dated May 18, 1928, says: "An investigation is under way to determine what befell Ambrose Bierce, noted author and journalist, who disappeared in Mexico in 1913, when the Southern Republic was in the revolutionary grip of Francisco Villa, the bandit leader. Mrs. Helen Isgrigg of Hollywood, the daughter of Bierce, announced last night that Colonel C. J. Vekardi of the Mexican Army has written her that he is having a measure of success in clearing up the mystery."

In one of his stories Bierce remarks: "To know that a man is dead should be enough." But we do not *know* that Bierce is dead!

Ambrose Bierce once told Ruth Guthrie Harding an anecdote about himself that should stand at the head of any discussion of his peculiarities: "A bystander, hearing an order given a mail clerk at a desk in a hotel, hurried across the lobby. 'I heard the name "Bierce"', he said, catching up at last with the man he was following. 'Do you know Ambrose Bierce?' Ambrose turned and looked down at him for a steady solemn instant; and in a gentle voice replied, 'No!' When he told me this, he lifted one eyebrow and chuckled. 'You ought,' I said, 'to be ashamed of yourself!' 'Well,' he answered, 'I don't know me, do I?'"

If Bierce didn't know himself certainly no one else has ever succeeded in thoroughly comprehending him. He was a mass of contradictions. Take one side of his character and use it as a basic element and you will go hopelessly astray. Unfortunately partial views of him have proved irresistibly attractive to those of his admirers who prefer to think of him as a permanent obscurian and who have made him a "cult" author. They have fostered the story of his being "Bitter" Bierce and have elaborated a legend of his character from that adjective. But Bierce's bitterness was to a very great extent impersonal. Fundamentally, he was serene.

Even disappointment did not destroy his serenity. He was forced to devote nine tenths of his energies to newspaper writing, which he regarded as a low occupation. His contributions to literature were ignored or despised by his generation. His books never sold. Even an extremely limited collected edition was disposed of with difficulty. Yet he rationalized even his rejection in a manner conducive to mental peace and calm. "If you stay in the game," he wrote in his essay on suicide, "which you are not compelled to do, take your losses in good temper and do not whine about them. They are hard to bear, but that is no reason why you should be."

Indeed, even in his old age, when his troubles weighed heavily upon him, he managed to remain calm. He never lost his amazingly high respect for literature. It was always a pleasure for him to write a meticulous criticism of a friend's manuscript. He chose the field of his final endeavours with the utmost calm. It was at this time that he found the hero of Upton Sinclair's *The Journal of Arthur Sterling* to be an impossible ass, quite the contradiction of all that an artist should be, particularly an artist of genius. He was considering this book when he wrote George Sterling his opinion on the serenity of genius: ". . . If genius is not serenity, fortitude and reasonableness I don't know what it is. One cannot even imagine Shakespeare or Goethe bleeding over his work and howling when 'in the fell clutch of circumstance.' The great ones are figured in my mind as ever smiling—a little sadly at times, perhaps, but always with conscious inaccessibility to the pinpricking little Titans that would storm their Olympus with ineffectual disasters and popgun misfortunes."

Yet Bierce was the victim of an ambivalence that made it quite impossible for him to live as calmly as his written statements would lead one to expect. He was a man whose emo-

tional life was highly developed and who felt
that it was his constant duty to guard it from
finding expression. His head made constant
war on his emotions—on his heart. As will be
shown later on, it was one of his fundamental
beliefs that the emotions were to be distrusted.
He demanded that they be severely restrained,
disciplined, and reduced to the positions of
servants of the intellect. Since he was of a
highly emotional nature it was very difficult
for him to follow this programme in his life.
In his writings he succeeded somewhat better,
for he could exercise a more severe censorship
over the written word than over his acts. It
is wrong, consequently, to put him down as
an unemotional man just because his writings
point in that direction.

To what extraordinary extremes he would
carry his dictatorship of the head we have
seen, and will see again in discussing his ideas
about a good life. Although he almost made a
cult of the idea of friendship he failed signally
as a friend, just because, as he put it, he carried

his ideas into his personal relationships with people. In other words, he allowed his head to dominate in matters that are best left chiefly to the heart. It was a mistake, but one that was brought about by his profound distrust of the emotions. Perhaps that distrust originated from the distressing failure of his marriage.

Just how seriously we are to take his brother Albert's diagnosis of his habit of hoarding up slights, real and imaginary, until the time came when he thought it necessary to release the full accumulation of bile, I do not know. That the habit existed is beyond doubt, and it certainly was a weakness of character of a major sort. It assisted to make him a "difficult" person. We know from written evidence of a few cases where the explosion that followed on long months of hoarding up his emotions was quite unjustified. We may assume that there are hundreds of other cases where his anger was equally unwarranted. Undoubtedly his furious anger against individuals who had nothing to do with him personally was rooted in this same emotional quirk. He ran counter to his own notions about serenity many times.

A good many people have attributed his actual and reputed bitterness to the fact that he felt defeated by life. Now, as I have tried to show, most of his bitterness was due to emotional instability. In his calmer moments he was not a bitter man. As I see it, the defeat he sustained worked out in quite another way than personal bitterness. It took the form of hampering his utterance. He left his work half done; his thoughts half expressed; his capacity for fiction only partly carried to fruition. As I shall have occasion to emphasize this point later it is not necessary to discuss it at length here. As he grew older he may have regretted that he had been so shortsighted as to allow his "parish and his time" to stop him from expanding and developing every part of his work. His regret, since regret may be closely allied to the emotions, may have been tinged with bitterness.

BITTER BIERCE

To the student his failure to carry out his work is quite understandable. Only a few authors are so intensely interested in what they are about as to carry on their work without the encouragement of an audience. Bierce was not an author of that sort. Furthermore, the encouragement he did get seems to me to have been of the wrong sort. It was too approving. This may seem nonsense in the face of his failure to make any impression on the public at large, but if one stops to consider that the public greeted his work with silence it will make my meaning apparent. Most of the vocal response he got was approving. When it was not, it was usually mere vituperation. In one of his letters Bierce says that most of his detractors were men of an inferior sort. That is a very significant statement, for it gives evidence of the fact that he was not conscious of the fact that he ever met an opponent worthy of his mettle. Dr. P. H. Boynton has pointed out that it was unfortunate that Bierce never had intellectual sparring

partners worthy of him. I think that opinion
is very true. Too many men followed James
Whitcomb Riley's tactics and answered Bierce
with "a large chunk of silence." It seems to me
that Bierce was the sort of man who would
have thriven on intelligent opposition.

Another thing that made it impossible for
Bierce to reach his full stature was the fact
that he was at odds with his environment all
the time. He was a perfectionist at a time
when public morals were very low and private
morals were nine tenths hypocrisy. He set up
a high code of morality and judged all men by
their deviation from it. He was an aristocrat
when democracy was an unquestioned dogma.
He saw the benefits that could arise from trusts
at a time when the intellectuals of America
were engaged in muckraking. He was opposed to labour unions when it was fashion-
able in intellectual circles to support them.
On the other hand, his position toward trusts
and labour unions did not make him popular
among the capitalists because of his distaste,

expressed in no uncertain terms, for the personnel of American business. In literature he was opposed to all the dominant trends and to all who supported them. It is, in fact, almost impossible to find a single topic upon which Bierce agreed with the general run of intellectuals of his day. He was a completely lone wolf. Naturally, then, he was left pretty much to himself. He could not even imagine a public for his ideas and consequently felt small urge to bring them to full expression. In this sense he was defeated by his time.

Fortunately he recognized that the public had rights, and one of them was the right to hit back when it was hurt. He did think, however, that it should have found a better way of replying to him than that of maintaining a dignified silence. He knew, too, that the public was in no way obligated to pay attention to a man just because he chose to set himself up as a writer. He knew the risks, and he was not embittered because he failed to make the grade, so to speak. When a contemporary

journalist wrote that Bierce was a man embittered by failure and so accounted for
his onslaughts upon men and things, Bierce
replied: "Without inquiring in what my failures have consisted, nor by what inspiration
my biographer knows what it is that I am trying to accomplish in this little life, I will let
that stand without comment; and carrying in
my soul this touching picture of a heart-broken
cynic, glittering with tears in the consciousness
that nobody but God loves him, yet smiling
through his hair as he feels upon his chin the
plash of other tears than his, I back away from
that sacred scene, and bidding myself a silent
farewell, fall first upon my knees, and then
upon my fools." Bierce's own comments on
the rewards of authorship are best summed
up in his remark about conditions in Ug, a
country he visited in his travels in the Land
Beyond the Blow: "The literature of Ug is
copious and of high merit, but consists altogether of fiction—mainly history, biography,
theology and novels. Authors of exceptional

excellence receive from the state marks of signal esteem, being appointed to the positions of laborers in the Department of Highways and Cemeteries."

And finally, a good deal of the talk about Bierce being bitter as a result of his failure to win general success as an author is founded on the false idea that a cynic is necessarily an unhappy man. He is apt, in fact, to take a great joy in the spectacle of life as it appears to his acrid vision. There is a sharp distinction between disillusion and despair. The great cynical humorists have not been the great despairers. The latter are usually lacking in humour and wit and all capacity for civilized living. Bierce was cynical—that is beyond question—but that he was unhappy does not seem to me true until we get to the last years of his life. When we get to those years we see him solving his troubles by returning to the situation that came nearest to corresponding to the happiest period in his life—for the Civil War he substituted the

Mexican Revolution. He sought consolation in action.

Van Wyck Brooks has written with great insight about this whole matter. He says: "No man was ever freer from personal bitterness . . . he was a starved man; but certainly it can be said that, if his generation gave him very little, he succeeded in retaining in his own life the poise of an Olympian."

Nevertheless, Bierce advised young authors to cultivate the good opinion of squirrels.

PART II
LITERATURE

INTRODUCTORY: HIS THEORIES

IN CONSIDERING Bierce's contributions to American literature it is necessary to keep in mind the fact that ninety per cent. of his energy went into journalism. In spite of the fact that Percival Pollard found him to be "the only American, living in America, who was completely a man of letters, in the finest sense of that term . . ." circumstances forced him into a position in which he could only rarely utilize either his creative or his satiric powers for the production of literature. Indeed, Arnold Bennett believes that journalism intruded itself even upon Bierce's so-called literary contributions to their detriment. For two thirds of his active life Bierce was engaged in a type of journalism that was not at all disagreeable

to him. Personal journalism throve on the
Pacific Coast from the days of the gold rush
to the 'nineties, and it gave Bierce full scope
for his extraordinary delight in prodding individuals. It was when the modern impersonal
style began to effect his life that he became
unhappy in newspaper work. Nevertheless,
whether pleasing to him or not, he made a
sharp distinction between journalism and literature. Journalism, he wrote, "is so low a
thing that it *may* be legitimately used as a
means of reform or a means of anything
deemed worth accomplishing. . . . Literature
is an *art;* . . . it is not a form of benevolence.
It has nothing to do with 'reform,' and when
used as a means of reform suffers accordingly
and unjustly." There is probably not another
writer in American literature who had so high
an ideal of literature as Bierce. It is probable,
too, that few writers ever found the practice of
their day so low and despicable. In presenting
Bierce's ideas on this or any other topic it is
necessary to give an exposition of his view

of actuality as well as of his view of the ideal.
The two are always diametrically opposed.

Bierce found himself a complete outsider
in the literary world of his day. He did not
accept the novel, realism, local colour, or slang.
He resisted the environmental pressure that
was making American literature deficient in
heartiness. On his side in this particular com-
bat he found Goethe, Shakespeare, Cervantes,
Molière, and Rabelais and was satisfied. He
despised magazine fiction and poetry through
their whole range. He was at odds with every
critic who supported the contemporary situation. He once lapsed into Johnsonese and called
the critics "microcephalus bibliopomps." As
a coat of arms for American letters he proposed
an illiterate hoodlum rampant on a field of
dead authors: motto, "To Hell with Literature."

His inability to find much of anything hope-
ful in contemporary literature produced a
terrific reaction and resulted in his amazing
portrait of literature as he conceived it to be

practised. Starting from the tools of authorship and working up, he damned everything. To begin with: "Quill, *n.* An imple-
ment of torture yielded by a goose and commonly wielded by an ass. This use of the quill
is now obsolete, but its modern equivalent,
the steel pen, is wielded by the same everlast-
ing Presence." The pen is chiefly in the hands
of those more suitably employed at the
plough. "Ink, *n.* A villainous compound of
tanno-gallate of iron, gum arabic and water,
chiefly used to facilitate the infection of idiocy
and promote intellectual crime." A pen dipped
in ink and applied to paper produced a manuscript which in due course came before an
editor who was "the trouble with American
literature." If it passed his inspection it fell
victim to a publisher. Now of all the people
Bierce hated none were hated more intensely
than the publishers. He developed his thesis
against them at length.

"What is a publisher? One of the most
famous definitions affirms him to be a person

who drinks champagne out of the skulls of
authors. Naturally that is an author's definition. The world has accepted it for its wit,
with a mental reservation taking account
of its probable untruth. Publishers having control of types and printing presses, and being
thriftily addicted to the maintenance of magazines and other periodicals to affirm their virtues and acclaim their wares, have pushed
themselves into public repute as a kind of
beings indubitably superior to such sordid
considerations as control the acts of merely
human tradesmen—children of light, whose
motives come of inspiration from Heaven, or
are the natural outgrowth of a native nobility
of soul fertilized by a generous desire to elevate the literary art. If authors have commonly indulged themselves in a different view
of the matter after some little experience,
they have not always taken the trouble to
avow it, or avowing it, to back up the avowal
with facts in justification. To eminent authors
whose words have most weight the publishers

have commonly made ample atonement for
their early sins against them; and authors obscure, besides not having access to the world's
ears, and being prevented by publishers from
reaching such ears as might be open to their
objurgations, are properly thought a pretty
testy lot anyhow. So it occurs that of all who
know publishers best, themselves are the only
persons bearing public witness of their works
and ways. And, God bless them; how they lie!

"Let it be understood that I write of book
publishers only, and of them in a general way;
of the genus, not of the few noble freaks due to
what the evolutionists call accidental variations. I fancy, too, that I write with some
knowledge of the subject, both old and new,
but the reader must fit me out with such an
equipment of motives as may best meet his
instinctive sense of the probabilities: I am
hardly likely to state any facts giving him
good ground for assumptions of personal
prejudice. With this confession to guard and
guide him he must be a very erratic reader

indeed—a constitutional and irreclaimable estray—if he permit me to mislead him.

"What, then, is a publisher? He is a person who buys of a small class of fools something which he sells to a large class of other fools. It is perhaps not surprising that he grows rich while the persons of whom he buys remain poor. The persons to whom he sells are not materially affected in fortune, for they buy but a little each; they are fools only in the sense of preferring worthless goods. Commonly he is a man of meagre education, having but little knowledge of what he buys and absolutely no more care for the interests of those producing it than a grain dealer for the interests of the farmer. Not so much; for the grain dealer knows that the bankrupt farmer may intermit production for a season while undergoing transformation to a tenant of his mortgagee, whereas the poorer an author becomes the most certainly and diligently he will make manuscript. In short, the transactions between author and publisher are on a purely commercial basis—that is to say, the one who has the whip hand of the situation 'cinches' the other all he knows how. It would hardly be necessary to say this but for a vague notion in the public mind that the goods changing hands are of a character to refine and ennoble somewhat the relations between sellers and buyers, and if the latter had not from immemorable time promoted that erroneous view: Production of literature that is good for anything but to sell does somewhat refine and ennoble the producer doubtless, or, rather, perhaps, persons of refinement and nobility are somewhat more likely to produce it, but I do not think its purchase and publication is regarded by the angels as a means of grace for subduing the soul of the publisher to godliness and purging it of thoughts of theft.

"Let us see what an author may reasonably hope to get by concession of these gracious gentlemen if he prefers to follow the appointed order of things by publishing first and becoming 'famous' afterward. (When comfortably famous, his name on the lips of every blackguard in the land, he may reverse the situation and bring the publisher to *his* terms.) The 'regular' rate to unknown, obscure, or only fairly popular authors, is ten per cent. of the retail price of each book sold. Let us now inquire in what relation to the project of publication this places the two parties to the transaction. Journalism being the profession that is least unlike that of literature may fitly be chosen to supply the 'standard of wages' for use here. Newspaper writers make from one thousand to ten thousand dollars a year; two thousand will serve our purpose well enough as a sum that a writer's time is worth. The most impetuous and prolific novelists with whom Heaven has had the goodness to bless us seldom bring forth more than one whelp at a time—produce more than one book a year is what I mean to say.

"The author of the book-to-be then, may be considered to have risked two thousand dollars on it to have put that sum into the enterprise. The publisher, venturing to print a small edition, puts in one half that amount. Let us be liberal, and counting in expenses of distribution, advertising, etc., say an amount just equal. But in dividing the proceeds, the publisher takes out of every dollar ninety cents and hands over ten cents to the author and then the good man executes upon the horn of him a lively fanfaronade in celebration of his generosity in consenting to exist.

"It is readily admitted that the cost of the manuscript to the author in time and labor is a matter with which the publisher has nothing to do, and which cannot with advantage be considered. In the matter, as to others, our old friend the law of supply and demand puts in a claim to consideration. But inasmuch as his reign is not altogether despotic, as is shown in the arbitrary adoption of ten per cent. as the author's rightful share, it seems not entirely unreasonable to hope that some-day an honest and intrepid publisher may defy the laws of supply and demand, break through the iron traditions of the trade, and commending his soul to God give as much as eleven."[1] It was the publisher's duty to have the manuscript put into type, "pestilent bits of metal suspected of destroying civilization and enlightenment." The proof reader in handling the copy "atones for making your writing nonsense by permitting the compositor to make it unintelligible." Released to the world, a book falls to a critic, "a person who boasts himself hard to please because nobody tries to please him." The total result is zero.

Extending his analysis from the mechanical aspects of authorship and publication, he was similarly vehement in his attacks upon the literary currents of the day. First and foremost he was opposed to the intrusion of a "purpose" into literature, although he did admit that the

[1] I have cited this somewhat fly-blown diatribe at length for two reasons: (1) It illustrates Bierce's reactions to the publishers of his day; and (2) it illustrates the type of argumentation with which he regaled the Californians in his column, "Prattle." It appeared in "Prattle" some time in May, 1892. I have cited it from Percival Pollard's *Their Day in Court*.

work of talented reformers was "better of course than the work of men of truer art and inferior brains." Nevertheless, his hostility was implacable. Apropos Tolstoy (whose genius he was among the first in America to recognize) and the reformers he wrote: "They are 'missionaries,' who, in their zeal to lay about them, do not scruple to seize any weapon that they can lay their hands on; they would grab a crucifix to beat a dog. The dog is well beaten, no doubt . . . but note the condition of the crucifix!" In denouncing the proponents of local colour he was similarly vigorous. He had nothing but contempt for the proposition that writing gains in merit by being "racy of the soil." "The writer," he said flatly, "who knows no better than to try to make his work 'racy of the soil' knows nothing of his art worth knowing." And on the use of dialect to contribute to this end he was similarly emphatic. He did, however, find that on certain occasions dialect could be used without giving offence. "With regard to dialect, the literary

law, I take it, is about this: To be allowable
in either verse or speech, not only of the
characters using it, but of the writer himself,
who, also, must be unable to write equally well
in the larger tongue. . . . In humorous and
satirical work like, for example, *The Biglow
Papers*, the law is relaxed, even suspended;
and in serious prose fiction if the exigencies
of the narrative demand the introduction of
an unlettered hind whose speech would naturally be 'racy of the soil' he must needs come
in and sport the tangles of his tongue. But he
is to be got rid of as promptly as possible—
preferably by death. The making of an entire
story out of the lives and loves and lingoes
of him and his co-pithecans—that is effron-
tery. If it be urged in deprecation of this my
view that it is incompatible with relish of and
respect for Miss Mary Wilkins Freeman, Miss
Mary Murfree, Mr. Hamlin Garland and
other curled darlings of the circulating li-
braries, I candidly confess that it is open to
that objection. Of all such offenders against

sweetness and sense I have long cherished a comfortable conviction that it were better if instead of writing things 'racy of the soil' they would till it. . . . The talk of intelligent persons in an unfamiliar language is a legitimate literary 'property,' but the talk of ignorant persons misusing their own language has value and interest to nobody but other ignorant persons and, possibly, the philologist. Literature, however, is not intended for service in advancing the interests of philology. The 'general reader' whose interest in the characters of a tale is quickened by their faulty speech may reasonably boast that the ties of affinity connecting him with their intellectual condition have not been strained by stretching: it is not overfar from where he is to where he came from." It is only a step from the use of dialect to the use of slang. Bierce was a fierce enemy of slang. "Slang is a foul pool at which every dunce fills his bucket, and then sets up as a fountain." Or slang is "the grunt of the human hog (*Pignoramus intolerabilis*) with an audible memory." He predicated his prediction that his *Devil's Dictionary* would not sell on the fact that "it has no slang, no 'dialect' and no grinning through a horse-collar."

Not content with having thrown overboard three major trends of his time, local colour, dialect, and slang, Bierce broadened his attack to include the novel. "A novel," he wrote with his usual dogmatism, "is a snow plant; it has no root in the permanent soil of literature, and does not long hold its place. It is the lowest form of imagination—imagination chained to the perch of probability. . . . It is a diluted story—a story cumbered with trivialities and nonessentials. I have never seen one that could not be bettered by cutting out half or three quarters of it. . . . Contemporary novels are read by none but the reviewers and the multitude—men of sane judgment and taste still illuminate their minds and warm their hearts in Scott's suffusing glow; the strange, heartless shimmer of Hawthorne fascinates more and more; the *Thousand and One Nights* holds its captaincy of tale telling. . . . Whatever a great man does he is likely to do greatly, but had Hugo set the powers of his giant intellect to the making of mere novels his superiority to the greatest of those who have worked in that barren art might have seemed somewhat less measureless than it is." More specifically, the novel is "a short story padded. A species of composition bearing the same relation to literature that the panorama bears to art. As it is too long to be read at a sitting the impressions made by its successive parts are successively effaced, as in the panorama. Unity, totality of effect, is impossible; for besides the few pages last read all that is carried in mind is the mere plot of what has gone before. To the romance the novel is what photography is to painting. Its distinguishing principle, probability, corresponds to the literal actuality of the photograph and puts it distinctly into the category of reporting. . . . The art of writing novels, such as it was, is long dead everywhere except in Russia, where it is new. Peace to its ashes—some of which have a large sale."

In Bierce's mind the novel was identified with realism, which he also despised. Realism, in his view, grew out of man's preoccupation with man, a quite unworthy preoccupation. "We human insects, as a rule, care for nothing but ourselves, and think that is best which most closely touches such emotions and sentiments as grow out of our relations, the one with another. I don't share this preference and a few others do not, believing that there are things more interesting than men and women." Realism logically became "the art of depicting nature as it is seen by toads. The charm suffusing a landscape painted by a mole, or a story written by a measuring-worm." That opinion needs no bush.

Of poetry Bierce's opinions were no less opposed to the dominant current. He once defined poetry as "a form of expression peculiar to the Land beyond the Magazines." Though

he persistently tried, he despaired of ever
finding a magazine editor who would recognize poetry when he saw it, let alone publish
it. Always an extreme purist, he placed great
emphasis on exact rhymes and traditional
forms. Lyric verse was an especial favourite
of his, and he demanded that it have tears in
it. As he was theoretically in favour of the
short story, so he was convinced that a poem
must be short. "I hold with Poe that there is
no such thing as a long poem—a poem of the
length of an Epic. It must consist of poetic
passages connected by *recitativo;* to use an
opera word. . . . If the writer cannot write 'sustained' poetry the reader probably could not
read it." Yet his views of verse were reasonably broad—broader certainly than on fiction.

It is obvious that Bierce eliminated many of
the elements in literature that make for popular appeal, and he certainly eliminated all the
elements that might have won him a contemporary audience. That he had so small a
contemporary audience is certainly not a

mystery. His "wise-cracks" on the authors and literature of his day are endless. "Platitude, *n.* The fundamental element and special glory of popular literature." "Serial, *n.* A literary work, usually a story that is not true, creeping through several issues of a newspaper or magazine. Frequently appended to each installment is a 'synopsis of preceding chapters' for those who have not read them, but a direr need is a synopsis of succeeding chapters for those who do not intend to read *them.* A synopsis of the entire work would be still better." "Tzetze (or Tsetse) Fly, *n.* An African insect (*Glossina morsitans*) whose bite is commonly regarded as nature's most efficacious remedy for insomnia, though some patients prefer that of the American novelist (*Mendax interminabilis*)." "Usage, *n.* The First Person of the literary Trinity, the Second and Third being Custom and Conventionality. Imbued with a decent reverence for this Holy Triad an industrious writer may hope to produce books that will live as long as the fashion."

BITTER BIERCE

Rejecting violently the novel, realism, dialect, and all use of slang, humorous or otherwise, Bierce stood firmly for the short story, romance, and pure English produced through intense, self-conscious discipline. Bierce was first and foremost a disciplinarian. He placed great emphasis on the technique of fiction and verse. He was constantly eager to be correct, and to see that others were correct even in the details of punctuation. More than anything else he sought precision in every part of composition, from the placing of the commas to sentence structure, to the finished whole. Yet however much he emphasized the technique of writing he was not an æsthetician. He scoffed at the idea that in writing a story an author solved any "æsthetic problem."

To achieve his ideal of a thoroughly equipped writer Bierce proposed a long, carefully thought out training. He had four objectives in view: (1) completely to deracinate his writer; (2) to bring the emotions under the control of the intelligence (He did not, as has been asserted many times, seek to destroy the emotions.); (3) to bring the imagination under control; and (4) to give his subject complete control over the mechanics of expression. On certain phases of this programme he wrote in this hyperbolical fashion: ". . . chiefly this fortunate youth with the brilliant future should learn to take comprehensive views, hold large convictions, and make wide generalizations. He should, for example, forget that he is an American and remember that he is a Man. He should be neither Christian, nor Jew, nor Buddhist, nor Mahometan, nor Snake Worshipper. To local standards of right and wrong he should be civilly indifferent. In the virtues, so-called, he should discern only the rough notes of a general expediency; in fixed moral principles only time-saving pre-decisions of cases not yet before the court of conscience. Happiness should disclose itself to his enlarging intelligence as the end and purpose of life; art and love as the only means to happiness. He should free himself of all doctrines, theories, etiquettes, politics, simplifying his life and mind, attaining to clarity with height. To him a continent should not seem wide nor a century long. And it would be needful that he know and have an ever present consciousness that this is a world of fools and rogues, consumed with vanity, selfish, false, cruel, cursed with illusions—frothing mad." But even with all that behind him, this youth would still be at the beginning of his career. "When my pupil should have had two years of this he would be permitted to try his 'prentice hand at a pig story in words of one syllable. And I should think it very kind and friendly if Mr. George Sylvester Vierick would consent to be the pig."

But one must get beyond pigs. What an author should deal with is discoverable from an account of Bierce's own interests. Bierce rejected the novel and realism to embrace romance. "The free wing of the romancer enables him to mount to such altitudes of the imagination as he may be fitted to attain; and the first three essentials of the literary art are imagination, imagination, and imagination. He can represent life, not as it is, but as it might be; character, not as he finds it, but as he wants it to be." Bierce's rejection of realism and acceptance of romance was based upon his fundamental distaste for the reality he found himself immersed in and his abhorrence of human character as it exhibited itself to him. How deep was his disgust for his environment can be illustrated by his remark: "Heaven is a prophecy uttered by the lips of despair, but Hell is an inference from analogy." In his own work in romance Bierce dealt principally with three topics—war, the supernatural, and religion. With the exception of the last each was handled in the short-story form. His philosophy of the short story was similar to that of Poe. He sought, like Poe, to make a single vivid impression upon the reader. To that end he eliminated all extraneous references. Furthermore, each story is a complete world in itself, controlled by the writer's logic, not by the illogicality of life. Since Bierce saw no point in reproducing the flat tones of ordinary life, he found an interesting topic only in the impingement of the extraordinary or the unreal on the normal course of events. This may be illustrated by his war stories. With no effort at selection to prove a point, five themes may be cited: a soldier on one side in the course of duty knowingly shoots down his father who is serving on the other; the adventures of a deaf and mute child on a battlefield; self-sought death provoked by idle gossip in a letter from a sweetheart; shelling in the course of duty one's own house, containing one's wife and child; and excessive daring as a reaction against congenital cowardice ending in apparent suicide by swinging. Nevertheless, it was Bierce's peculiar power to make these unusual happenings seem as vivid and real as the most "true-to-life" stories recorded by professed realists. As has been pointed out, these extraordinary happenings always impinged on ordinary life. And ordinary life did not need to be distorted by their introduction. War, of course, is a departure from the ordinary, but Bierce's ghost stories are all attached to life in times of peace, and the outstanding merit of Bierce's picture of war is its extraordinary reality!

A man with such a penchant for dogmatism as Bierce would naturally make a poor critic. Although admirable for the cogency with which they were reasoned, his opinions so narrowed his perceptions as to make his work in this department chiefly a matter of defence of his own point of view and offence against those who violated his dogmas. Though he occasionally wrote an essay against a literary trend into which he introduced names, Bierce never wrote an extended essay on any literary figure of whom he approved or disapproved. Aside from his reasoned defence of his own type of art he was singularly deficient in critical capacity in the larger sense. With a lapse in logic quite unusual with him he asserted in an essay that "In literary criticism there are no criteria, no accepted standards of excellence by which to test the work," and a few paragraphs later laid down the dogma that "the universal and immutable laws of art were known to Aristotle and Longinus"! Believing as he did, in the force of heredity he naturally rejected the sociological theory of art that gives environment a determining place in the formation of art values. He apparently believed that an artist creates his work *in vacuo*. Fortunately he realized his own deficiencies. He did not set up as a critic. He saw that ". . . the critic's theories are imposed by his own limitations." Nevertheless, recognition of that fact did not prevent him from assaulting any and all writers who dissented from his position. Other than that his criticism usually consisted of word usage and such questions. He rarely went below the surface.

Where he got his notions about art is difficult to say. Partly, as was suggested earlier,

they may have been the result of his own tre-
mendous reaction against the sordid times
and people with which he dealt as a journalist.
Partly they may have come from a study of
Longinus and Aristotle, though personally, I
am skeptical of the profundity of Bierce's culture. Certainly his notions of style can be
traced directly to influences that worked upon
him during his English sojourn. He always
recommended Spencer's essay on style to beginning writers and suggested a study of the
prose of Walter Savage Landor. On the surface it would seem logical to believe that his
philosophy of the short story, of poetry, and
of romance was taken over bodily from Poe,
but Bierce resented that suggestion during his
lifetime. He asserted that the agreement was
accidental and that critics who said that he
was an offshoot of Poe were simply too ignorant to know that similar ideas could be originated from quite dissimilar sources and by
men who had never heard of each other. The
whole question is as vexed as that the anthro-

pologists have on their hands: are cultural
identities and similarities the result of separate
inventions sometimes produced by quite different convergences in development, or did
they originate at one point and become dif-
fused by contacts immediate or remote?

The question of the extent of Bierce's culture is even more difficult. It largely depends
on whether one is favourably disposed to him
or not. One thing seems certain to me, and
that is that however much he may have read
none of it ever became an integral part of his
mind. He may have been, as Mr. Eric Patridge
believes, intimately acquainted with the older
English writers like Morryster, Denneker,
and Glanvill; with the English poets, Shakespeare, Milton, Coleridge, Pope, Dryden, and
Keats; with the English prose writers, Defoe,
Swift, Scott, and Thackeray; with Hugo,
Goethe, Heine, Omar Khayyám, Homer,
Plato; the Greek dramatists, Virgil, Horace,
and Juvenal. He undoubtedly was acquainted
with some of these writers, but how intimately

it is impossible to know. The records available do not show. In addition he had read Voltaire and Tolstoy. He knew the works of Poe, Hawthorne, Longfellow, and Whittier, but seemingly did not have a wide knowledge of American literature, historical or contemporary. The impression one gets is that in his busy life he never had time to acquire a thorough grounding in any department of literature or in the literature of any country. If he had, it would be impossible to feel, as every reader of Bierce must, that he was culturally a starved man. His whole work might have been written, not by a man who had never read a line, but certainly by a man whose chief assets were a capacity for acute critical observation and a gift of cogent expression.

Nor was he better equipped in other fields. His knowledge of the theatre was negligible. He did not have an ear for music at all. And Percival Pollard found his views on painting not worth considering. He had small understanding of the fundamentals of economics and sociology, although his observations and logical deductions were amazingly keen. Politics he knew from observation. In general it may be said that he failed to make an impression with his ideas as much because of lack of learning to sustain them as because they were heretical. That, however, does not discount their penetration.

Dr. Pattee in *The Development of the American Short Story* points out that Bierce's contribution to the evolution of the form was negligible. "When . . . one studies the history of the American short story evolution, not from the point of view of what might have been or what should have been, but of what actually happened, one is compelled to the conclusion that Ambrose Bierce was a vivid episode rather than a positive force. . . . In the school of the anecdotal short story, brilliant, witty, climactic, Bierce undoubtedly is a transition figure. The steps in the evolution of the form that seems to have culminated in the volumes of short story yearbooks edited by O'Brien, are, therefore, Harte and Aldrich, Matthews and Bunner, Ambrose Bierce and O. Henry." This is certainly not brilliant company for Bierce. He would undoubtedly have loathed Aldrich and Bunner and Matthews on the grounds that they were lacking in heartiness. Did he not speak with disgust of "Miss Nancy Howells" and "Miss Nancy James"? And would he not have extended that judgment to these much weaker sisters? As to O. Henry, to whom Bierce curiously enough never made reference, his distortions of the English tongue were sufficient to cause Bierce to slaughter him with infinite pleasure. Bierce must be classified with these men on one ground only: he used essentially the same form. The story by Bierce that most frequently appears in anthologies, "An Occurrence at Owl Creek Bridge," is a perfect example of the "snap ending," which in Aldrich's hands Howells found to be a new form of literary pleasure. But how far apart Bierce and Aldrich were in the use to which they put the form! Writing of Aldrich in the *American Mercury* for May, 1925, I pointed out: "On a framework as artificial as Aldrich's, Bierce has draped veracious observation and pessimistic, piercing philosophy. His style is as sparse and severe as Aldrich's, but it lacks the latter's weak prettiness, a prettiness having 'the tints of flowers without their sap and roots.' The resultant contrast appears in considering Bierce's 'A Horseman in the Sky' and Aldrich's 'White Feather.' The framework is the same, and both were inspired by the Civil War. A Southerner in the Northern army is called upon in the course of duty to shoot down a relative. Bierce concludes with an officer questioning a sentry who has fired and seems reluctant to say at what:

"'See here, Druse,' he said, after a moment's silence, 'it's no use making a mystery. I order you to report. Was there anybody on the horse?'
"'Yes.'
"'Well?'
"'My father.'

"The Sergeant rose to his feet and walked away. 'Good God!' he said.

But Aldrich, confronted with the identical situation, makes a previously brave man show the white feather and, after brooding a few days, commit suicide. Stylistically these men were near together; mentally they were miles apart."

Dr. Pattee discovers the connecting link between Bierce and O. Henry (and also retrospectively with Bret Harte) to be Bierce's story "The Famous Gilson Bequest." This unfortunate story is quite uncharacteristic of the mature Bierce and belongs with the impossible "California" jocosities that disfigured his London period. Bierce himself correctly evaluated it when he printed all the stories of a related nature that he included in his *Collected Works* under the title "Negligible Tales." They are—decidedly so.

Bierce's one connection with contemporary trends seems to be an unfortunate one. He chose a form for his stories that could quickly degenerate in the hands of lesser men, as it did. In his hands, however, it was carried to the highest possible pitch of excellence because it provided so excellent a channel for the realization of his fundamental literary ideals.

If Dr. Pattee, is right, O. Henry must be numbered among the writers who have felt Bierce's influence. Unfortunately it was on the lowest possible plane. An even more debatable case of Bierce's influence is that on Stephen Crane. Percival Pollard stated most emphatically: ". . . they [the critics Pollard disliked] praised that book [*The Red Badge of Courage*] out of all proportion to the debt it owed the Bierce book, which in artistry, towered so far above it." Bierce's own judgment of *The Red Badge* has been cited. I do not think there is much basis for Pollard's dogmatism. He was quite enamoured of Bierce and when another good book about the Civil War appeared he could not imagine how anybody but Bierce could be mentioned in connection

with that topic. Thomas Beer did not find that
Crane ever read Bierce.

In fact, Bierce's alleged influence on any
writer is to be viewed with considerable skepticism. He is not the sort of writer who has
"influence." And certainly Mr. Eric Patridge
strains my will to believe when he asserts that
Bierce "influenced Capek, for the central idea
of *R. U. R.* is explicit, and several of its important incidents are implicitly in 'Moxon's
Master,' while at other points of the play we
can indicate what look like developments from
suggestions made by Bierce." Perhaps someone will now arise to assert that Bierce's story
suggested Zamiatin's *We*. Or, for that matter, why not attribute the radio curse to
Bierce? In his satiric sketch "For the Ahkoond" he anticipates wireless telegraphy,
dubbing the imaginary instrument the iso-
chronophone.

Chapter 2

ON WAR

A GENERATION brought up on the fiction that has grown out of the Great War will find Bierce's war stories somewhat unsatisfying. They are very definitely old-fashioned in form, and he was not interested in presenting a comprehensive view of war as a variety of human experience. The nature of the form he chose for his stories has been discussed earlier and so have the types of themes that interested him. It is not necessary to go over that ground here. It is worth while, however, to point out that Bierce as fully comprehended the nature of war as the most realistic writer about the Great War.

Dr. Percy H. Boynton has pointed out that Bierce "turned naturally to war episodes, because, although actual, they were farthest

134

from the even tenor of normal life." That is part of the story. Another point to make is that the war was the one period of his life when he completely expressed his personality, and it gave him infinite pleasure to con it over. Though war was removed "from the even tenor of normal life," Bierce was not satisfied with that alone. He was interested only when the extraordinary impinged on the normal course of war. His war stories, therefore, are twice removed from ordinary life. Nevertheless, Bierce was supremely successful in visualizing the actualities of war, but he chose to cast his stories with extraordinary plots. Modern readers are struck by the realism of the trappings of his stories and annoyed by the "thrilling" plots. It is a contradiction that annoys them so much that they may fail to see how complete Bierce's realistic view of war really was.

Shortly before he died in 1920, William Dean Howells ventured a prediction. He was quite sure that war was so hostile to the creative artist that it was useless to hope for really great fiction about the World War. He recalled that nothing of particular importance, to his mind, had come out of the Civil War and asked, in the light of this, how one could have any optimism about the possible products of an infinitely more horrible war. Mr. Howells was forgetful. He failed to remember that the circumstances of life in the United States during the post-Civil War period made it exceedingly difficult for a creative artist to exist. He forgot that he himself had erected an æsthetic that excluded the treatment of subjects so brutal and horrible as war. He did not realize, of course, that his æsthetic was an escape from the difficulties of the creative life in the United States of his day. If he had he would have noted, taking a comprehensive view of the subject, that if someone had been able to find the leisure to write a realistic piece of fiction about the war there would have been but a very small sympathetic audience for it. The survivors of the Civil War who could put

their thoughts on paper apparently preferred
to regard the war through a halo of civilian
romance. Mr. Thomas Beer has looked into
this subject and in his unique manner has
summed up his conclusions: "The war left
almost nothing printed that the literate peas-
ants and clerks who fought would recognize
as the truth of their acts. In Cooke's *Mohun*
one finds a rather vivid picture of collapsing
Richmond with its intrigues, its profiteers and
its frantic pleasures. . . . He was honest and
not too extravagant but he was no realist.
There is no Northern fiction worth a glance. . . .
The realists sat on fences and the steps of
stores in the sprawled depth of the nation and
made a topic of the war when political campaigns and labour held no thrill. . . . In 1870
James Russell Lowell found that stories of the
battle line 'obscene and horrible' were being
told before young boys by the commonplace
veterans of Cambridge, Massachusetts, and
it is pretty evident that the realists on shady
corners preferred war in that form."

BITTER BIERCE

Bierce saved up his own view of the war until 1892, when *Tales of Soldiers and Civilians* appeared. The book caused scarcely a ripple. In 1896 *The Red Badge of Courage* came out, and for the first time a realistic view of the Civil War achieved popularity. But Crane dealt with war second-hand. Bierce seems to be about the only writer who fought in the Civil War who allowed truthful memories of the conflict to get onto paper. In that respect his stories are unique.

He took an unromantic view of war, but the machinery that he chose for his stories is, by his own definition, romantic. To get the full force of his observations it is necessary to separate his observations from the *effect* any particular story may make upon the reader. Bierce never had any particular interest in the issues of the war. A soldier rarely does. He believed that war was simply an instrument of national policy somewhat more violent and destructive than those resorted to in a political campaign but of no greater significance fundamentally. He knew that one of its most inportant functions was to revive the vice of patriotism. Though some of the writers of to-day seem to think that they are the first to do so, Bierce recognized that the soldiers had little feeling of hostility toward the enemy. He saw clearly enough that the really vindictive animosity was behind the lines. The soldier, he thought, regarded the enemy as a different order of beings from himself—a sort of extraordinarily wary animals he was engaged in stalking: "The soldier never becomes wholly familiar with the conception of his foes as men like himself; he cannot divest himself of the feeling that they are another order of beings, differently conditioned, in an environment not altogether of the earth." This is a feeling quite different from hatred. Reducing the matter to lowest terms, as he did every matter he analyzed, Bierce emphasized the fact that a soldier was not a defender of ideals but a "hardened and impenitent man-killer." From the opposite angle he was a man whose business it was to "face firearms with malevolent eyes blazing behind them." Even such an obvious contrast as that between the pageantry of war which appeals to the civilian and the actuality of war which bears down upon the soldier in the lines was announced as a discovery by fiction writers in recent times. It goes without saying that Bierce recognized and discussed this contrast. "Even in his distress and peril [he has been caught at the front by a sudden attack] the helpless civilian could not forbear to contrast it [the battle] with the gorgeous parades and brilliant uniforms, the music, the banners, and the marching. It was an ugly and sickening business: to all that was artistic in his nature, revolting, brutal, in bad taste."

Yet with all this the fact remains that Bierce's view of war "dates." There is an old-fashioned air about his stories. It is necessary to recognize that the Civil War was fought between eras in warfare, so to speak. It was fought just when the industrial revolution was making itself felt in this country. The mechanization of warfare was barely under way. If the technique of the Civil War, compared with that of the Revolution, is quite modern, compared to the World War the Civil War is definitely premechanical. Consequently the individual was not so far submerged in the Civil War as he was in the World War. The old-fashioned virtues of the soldier were allowed freer play. It was the last war that made a deep impression on the American people that allowed a chance for the expression of heroic gestures.

As we have seen and shall see again in greater detail, Bierce's virtues were essentially old-fashioned. Along with an exceedingly low view of mankind he entertained a moral code of the highest sort. Freed from the frauds and trickeries of civilian life, he believed that a man as soldier could follow this code and reap the reward of his idealism. Bierce did not view an army as a vast machine composed of submerged human units. He did not even recognize that to some men it might mean the crushing of all that was best in them. He saw war as high adventure even though it was hedged about with horrible accompaniments. In his view the virtues of a soldier were conscience and courage (without vanity), devotion and daring. He took particular pleasure in portraying deeds that illustrated these virtues. Nevertheless, he recognized that what is called courage may in essence be nothing but an extreme reaction from fear, and he was very sensitive to the fact that the most heroic gestures were empty and aimless as contributions to the real object of the campaign which always was to defeat the enemy. Furthermore, he knew that none of the virtues he admired were capable of surviving the strain of untoward circumstances.

Bierce's view of war, then, was essentially this: war was the last resort of conflicting national and international interests; it offered the individual escape from the base necessities of civilian life; in it the highest moral code could be followed by the soldiers; yet in its accompaniments it was horrible. This view of war is a mixture of the modern and the old-fashioned. Bierce's stories make the same mixed impression on the reader. In addition to juxtaposing the most horrible reality with the highest sort of human idealism, he further complicated matters by using, as has been pointed out, plots that strike us as artificial. Bierce was a romantic realist.

Bierce's war stories, contained in *In the Midst of Life* and *Can Such Things Be?* number but nineteen. With these nineteen stories he has made a reputation greater than that of any other American writer about war with the exception of Stephen Crane. Yet even within that narrow range Bierce was unable to keep from repeating himself. For instance, he played several variations on the idea of a soldier on one side shooting down, in the course of duty, near and dear relatives on the other. Even when we take the themes that he chose to treat, as was done in part earlier, we are struck by the fact that the plots are lacking in any extraordinary brilliance. It seems, therefore, quite just to say that Bierce was lacking in inventiveness. It is highly improbable that he put all he had to say about the war into nineteen brief stories. He did not go on, in all probability, simply because he could not find more extraordinary incidents to treat. This seems to me to reveal a fundamental weakness in his theory of art. It placed too much emphasis on mere inventiveness. It did not place enough emphasis on what seems to me the factor that makes fiction moving, the reflection of life through a contemplative consciousness. In the hands of a man whose inventiveness outran his capacity for observation and reflection the literary value of the products would quickly become negligible.

Of the nineteen stories about war that he wrote, four seem to me the best. They are: "A Horseman in the Sky," "An Occurrence at Owl Creek Bridge," "Chickamauga," and "One of the Missing." The rest seem to me to have varying degrees of merit, but these four contain all that is essential to an understanding of Bierce's view of war and also give one a clear notion of his skill as a story-teller. They all contain the following elements: trick plot, veridical observation, accurate psychology, and devastating emotional effect upon the reader.

An analysis of "One of the Missing" will make Bierce's methods more understandable to the reader of this discussion. It will also serve to emphasize again the fact that he was not so much interested in reproducing the actualities of war, which would be the central interest of the realists he despised, as in using the circumstances of war, with which he was familiar, as a setting for some unusual happening. It was always the extraordinary happening that provided his excuse for a story. That fact cannot be too frequently emphasized. Failure to recognize it has made more than one critic's discussion of Bierce quite irrelevant.

The chief character in "One of the Missing"

is Jerome Searing. He is described as an "incomparable marksman, young, hardy, intelligent, and insensible to fear." In addition he is possessed of extraordinary daring, a thorough knowledge of woodcraft, sharp eyes, and a truthful tongue. It is these qualities that have won him the position of spy. In this story he is detailed to get as close to the enemy's lines as possible, to determine the disposition of their forces. He finds that the enemy has withdrawn. Not satisfied with determining this essential fact he decides to observe further. He crawls into a dilapidated granary. Looking out through one of the gaps he sees the rear guard of the enemy still within reach of his rifle. Although completely aware of the fact that he cannot do any material harm and certainly no good by firing, he nevertheless determines to do so. He cocks his gun and takes aim.

Up to this point the story gives no indication of being more than a somewhat commonplace episode. Bierce, however, never stops with the commonplace. In this case he resorts to coincidence to precipitate the extraordinary happening that is to give point to the story. Coincidence was a favourite device with him. His weakness for it was as great as that of William Dean Howells. After a somewhat platitudinous dissertation on the idea that all is foreordained he gives us a glimpse of an enemy officer performing an act as idle as Searing's. "As it fell out, a Confederate captain of artillery, having nothing better to do while awaiting his turn to pull out and be off, amused himself by sighting a field-piece obliquely to his right at what he mistook for some Federal officers on the crest of a hill, and discharged it. The shot flew high of its mark." It hit the ramshackle granary in which Searing was hiding, and the building collapsed. Later we are told that this occurred at six eighteen o'clock. Searing finds himself caught in the timbers—absolutely trapped. He is unable to make a single move that will assist him to get free. After fruitlessly trying various expedients he is brought up short by the sudden realization that he is looking straight into the muzzle of his rifle. It is aimed at the centre of his forehead. He realizes, too, that just before the accident he had cocked his rifle. The moment he realizes his horrible predicament his morale begins to disintegrate. Thoughts of his wife and children, of his early boyhood, of his first days as a soldier flash through his mind. His head begins to throb, the exact point at which the rifle is aimed being the centre of the pain. There are periods when he is unconscious. In frenzy he slashes about aimlessly. Rats appear and look at him: ". . . the thought flashed into his bewildered mind that they might touch the trigger of his rifle, he cursed them and ordered them to go away. 'It's no business of yours,' he cried. The creatures went away; they would return later, attack his face, gnaw away his nose, cut his throat—he knew that, but he hoped by that time to be dead." This episode provides the touch of horror indispensable to a Bierce war story. He returns to the idea of animals gnawing dead bodies on the battlefields several times in his nineteen stories. It fascinated him.

Slowly Searing loses all balance and is mastered by animal fear. "Jerome Searing, the man of courage, the formidable enemy, the strong, resolute warrior, was pale as a ghost. His jaw was fallen; his eyes protruded; he trembled in every fibre; a cold sweat bathed his entire body; he screamed with fear. He was not insane—he was terrified." In desperation he tries to loosen a board with the idea of using it to deflect the bullet when the gun goes off. He fails because of his cramped position. The failure somewhat calms him. He deliberately plans suicide. Since he cannot loosen the board he pushes it slowly through the pile of débris until it rests against the trigger guard. He manipulates it so that with a shove he can make it hit the trigger, "then closing his eyes, he thrusts it against the trigger with all his strength! There was no explosion; the rifle had been discharged as it dropped from his hand when the building fell. But it did its work."

149

BITTER BIERCE

Bierce often used an epilogue to heighten his effects. He does so here. He was never averse to resorting to quite obvious tricks to accomplish his end. In this case Searing's brother commands the advance that follows the long silence in the Confederate lines. As the troops move forward he observes the body lying in the collapsed building. He notices that the dead man's uniform is gray. Searing's uniform is so covered with dust that a casual observer would mistake it for that of a Confederate soldier. He observes the body somewhat closely. "Its face is yellowish white; the cheeks are fallen in, the temples sunken, too, with sharp ridges about them, making the forehead forbiddingly narrow; the upper lip, slightly lifted, shows the white teeth, rigidly clenched. The hair is heavy with moisture, the face as wet as the dewy grass all about. From his point of view the officer does not observe the rifle; the man was apparently killed by the fall of the building. . . . 'Dead a week,' said the officer curtly, moving on and absently pulling out his watch as if to verify his estimate of time. Six o'clock and forty minutes." Standing behind the lines the rumble of the collapsing building had caused him idly to look at his watch at six-eighteen. In twenty-two minutes his brother, whose bravery was notorious, had so far been transformed by untoward circumstances as to die of fear in such a manner that his appearance underwent a complete transformation. He appeared to the eyes that knew him best like an unknown person who had been dead a week! /

This story tells us more directly than endless exposition can what is meant by the generalization that Bierce was only moved to write a story when he discovered a case where the extraordinary impinged upon the ordinary tenor of events. This is a typical Bierce story. Time and again, both in his war stories and in his tales of civilians, he returns to the idea that fear can transform an individual beyond recognition. It was the sort of thing that interested him. The irony of it pleased him.

Chapter 3

ON GHOSTS AND THE
SUPERNATURAL

ENOUGH has been said to make it obvious
why Bierce chose to write stories about supernatural happenings. Such happenings are romantic in essence. Furthermore, they provided
baffling problems for his analytic intelligence.
Can Such Things Be? he named the book that
contains most of his stories of the supernatural,
and the interrogative title implies both skepticism and credulity. Bierce apparently wished
to say, "I hardly believe these things, yet
here are actual reports made by veracious witnesses." In common with most persons of a
skeptical habit of mind he was fascinated by
the unusual and apparently inexplicable. On
occasion he would so plan a story that alongside the supernatural would run a rationalistic

152

explanation of the happening. More frequently he offered no explanation. His attitude toward one aspect of the supernatural, ghosts, is summed up in his definition of a ghost: "The outward and visible sign of an inward fear." Bierce believed that fear played a large part in psychic life. He was interested in ghosts as pragmatic and bizarre manifestations of a fundamental human characteristic. By this very fact his stories of ghosts gain in vividness and power.

In dealing with the supernatural Bierce was working in an American literary tradition of long standing. The supernatural has figured in American literary life since the time of Increase and Cotton Mather. It was only when belief in the reality of the supernatural declined, however, that the writers wove tales that have remained permanently interesting. The first purely literary utilization of the supernatural was by Charles Brockden Brown. He was followed by Washington Irving, Poe, Hawthorne, Fitz-James O'Brien, and Lafcadio

Hearn. Various writers of equal importance
have dealt with the supernatural incidentally,
and lesser writers owe what measure of permanent fame they have to some successful
handling of a supernatural theme. No writer
made the supernatural so exclusive an interest
as it was with Bierce. He alone was willing
to rest a reputation on so gruesome a basis.

Twenty themes that Bierce treated may be
cited as examples of the sort of topics that
fascinated his imagination. They are: the
accidental return to the unknown grave of a
loved one and there meeting death; sleeping by
accident in an eerie place and dreaming of a
gruesome happening that actually took place
there unknown to the sleeper; snatching the
body of a man who turns out to have been
buried alive; a mysterious disappearance
complicated by murder and amnesia; seeing
a ghost as a premonition of death; a horror
story of a mechanical man; a fight with a dead
body in the dark leading to death from fear;

uncanny happenings, the result of the mistaken identity of twins; a ghost that has returned to its customary occupations, seen by
one who knows nothing of the death; hallucina-
tions of an attack by a dog leading eventually
to death and the discovery of teeth marks on
the body; dreaming of happenings that subsequently were proved to be true; a study of
the effects of inherited fear; a conflict with an
invisible being; a ghost seen with equal vividness by a group of spectators; a study in te-
lepathy; a murderer captured by the ghost of
the warder he has killed in escaping from jail;
death from fear of a stuffed snake seen under
unusual circumstances; death from fear by one
who disbelieved in ghosts but who, in suitable
surroundings and with his mind occupied with
such matters, is induced to believe he has seen
a ghost, with an accompanying rational explanation of the whole happening; a study of
a haunted house; and a study of what is
apparently a contact with the spirit world.
Some of these themes were treated several

times; others but once. It will be noticed how
many of them have some obvious relation to
fear. Fear was Bierce's point of reference in all
of his discussions of supernatural happenings.
Many of these stories about the supernatural
have achieved such fame in themselves that
readers are familiar with them and know nothing about Ambrose Bierce or any of his other
writings. It would be easy to separate perhaps
a dozen that stand out as masterpieces, but I
do not intend to do so. It is a more important
matter to analyze four stories, all different in
theme, with a view to observing Bierce at
work. For this purpose I have chosen, and will
consider in order, "A Jug of Sirup," "The
Damned Thing," "The Death of Halpin
Frayser," and "Moxon's Master." They
should serve to illustrate all the points of interest about Bierce's work in this field.

"A Jug of Sirup." This story opens with an
elaborate exhibition of proofs that the central
character, Silas Deemer, actually died. From
that point it is concerned with the fact that he

came back as a ghost. To impress on the reader
the fact that locale is an important factor in
ghost stories it is Bierce's next concern to
establish the fact that Deemer was a man of
extremely fixed and orderly habits. Silas
Deemer kept the country store and for twenty-
five years, Sundays excepted, was never seen
any place other than behind his counter. To
heighten the impression of Deemer's regularity
of habits Bierce narrates an anecdote. Deemer
had been summoned to appear as a witness
in an important law case. He did not attend,
and when the lawyer who was interested in
his possible testimony asked the Court to ad-
monish him, the Court was surprised at this
presumption. It was impossible that anyone
should undertake to disturb Deemer's habits.
Not to disturb the orderly progress of his
business, Deemer died in the night. He was
duly buried as noted above, but within a
month he "made it plain that he had not the
leisure to be dead." Now it will have been
noticed that Bierce was not adverse to adopt-

ing a very roundabout way of telling a story. He has here started with a fact and then gone away around about to explain the fact. Once arrived at his starting point again the story proceeds.

Immediately after the sentence quoted Bierce starts on a new tack: "One of Hillbrook's most respected citizens was Alvan Creede, a banker." It is then carefully established that Creede is a man of substance and undoubted veracity. More than that, his business is such that he has made periodic visits to a neighbouring metropolis. He is not a mere hick. He is pictured arriving at his home about ten one moonlit night with a jug of sirup, so he thinks. His wife greets him in the front hall, and he turns to pick up the jug which he has set down on the veranda while he gets out his keys to open the door. It is not there. He invokes the Devil in his irritation. His wife asks if he is sure he had a jug. He then elaborates on his purchase of it from Deemer, but midway in his story he stops and staggers into the hallway and slumps down in a chair. He suddenly remembers that Deemer has been dead for three weeks.

The realization upon him that he has "seen a ghost," Creede tries to rationalize that happening but has only half succeeded in doing so when his little daughter, who has heard not a word of the monologue he has gone through, dashes in to be kissed good-night and asks, "Papa dear, Eddy says mayn't he have the little jug when it is empty?" His elaborate half-explanations crash to the ground. The jug was seen in his hand! Yet he knows perfectly well that Deemer is dead, and furthermore, once he stops to think of it, the stock of the store was sold *en bloc* to a competitor who has removed it to his own store. Deemer's family has moved away. The store is as much an unreality as Deemer. Yet Creede arrived home carrying a jug that he bought from Deemer.

The "ghost" established, Bierce then proceeds to make the hallucination a community affair. The next night, the story of Creede's

adventure having spread through the village,
a crowd gathers before the erstwhile Deemer's
erstwhile store. The crowd is in a half-
believing state of mind, but not a single member of it is brave enough to enter the vacant
store. The bravest will do no more than
rattle the door, throw stones at the building,
or challenge the ghost to a foot race. Suddenly
the store is filled with light that seems to
come from a candle. The crowd then observes
what it takes to be Silas Deemer at work on
his account book. The effect is magical. The
timid run away; the skeptical walk slowly
away; in the end there remain but "a score
or more, mostly men . . . speechless, staring
and excited."

Three of the braver spirits advance toward
the store and enter. They are heard knocking about inside, bumping into each other and
into empty boxes and barrels, cursing and
shouting. This does not have the slightest
effect on the composure of Silas Deemer. In
some manner unexplained the remainder of the

crowd is drawn into the building. To those inside, the store is in black darkness. The light is apparent only to the observer outside. Inside the scene is astonishing: "They groped with aimless imprecision, tried to force their way out against the current, and were trampled, rose and trampled in their turn. They seized one another by the garments, the hair, the beard—fought like animals, cursed, shouted, called one another opprobrious and obscene names." Once they were all in, the "light" went out. The one man who resisted the pull of this collective mania, Alvan Creede, turned and walked away.

The next day it was observed that the store had obviously been the scene of a terrific battle. An examination of the account book showed that the last transaction entered was for the day of Deemer's death!

"A Jug of Sirup" serves to illustrate certain characteristics of Bierce's ghost stories, psychological and technical. In the first place it shows that he was not adverse to telling a story in a somewhat roundabout way. Next, that he made every effort to make the setting as real as possible. Thirdly, it must be observed that he elaborated the testimony as the existence of the ghost from one individual who saw it by an inadvertence, so to speak, to a crowd of supposedly rational people. By starting with the testimony of one reliable observer he prepared the minds of the later spectators for the sight of a ghost. That releases the more or less repressed belief in ghosts that they have. This arranged he proceeds, fourthly, to break down their skepticism entirely and complete the atavistic reversion by drawing them by psychic contagion into the building where the ghost has been "seen" and there allowing them to give free rein to their terror. All the while he maintains an ironic and unbelieving attitude toward the whole occurrence in his manner of narrating the episode.

In other ghost stories Bierce relied more fully on fear to make the tale logical and maintained a more severely objective attitude

in the telling. Take "The Suitable Surroundings." In this story the narration is managed
in an even more roundabout manner, but the
idea is essentially this: A man who completely
disbelieves in ghosts accepts the challenge of
a writer of ghost stories to place him in a situation where he will see one. The challenge accepted, the writer provides the skeptic with a
particularly gruesome manuscript and directs
him to take it, after dark, to a reputedly
haunted house and read it by the light of a
candle. The skeptic does so and is engaged in
reading when a boy, out hunting stray cows,
notices the light in the deserted house. He
gets closer to see what is going on and sees the
man reading by the light of a candle. His face
white with fear, he nevertheless makes a su-
preme effort to observe the man closely and
puts his face close to the window. At that
moment the reader looks up, sees the white,
fear-drawn face, screams, knocks over the
candle, and falls down dead! Here again, be
it observed, Bierce is careful to provide for a

realistic background. He asks the reader to take nothing for granted. It is an objective account of what occurred. Believe it or not, the story tells what actually happened. Can such things be?

"The Damned Thing." This story bears some obvious relations to Fitz-James O'Brien's "What Was It?" In it Bierce has cleverly mixed the real and the supernatural to such a point that the reader is prepared to accept the supernatural as true. The story opens with a group of men sitting around a corpse waiting for a witness to arrive so that they may go on with the inquest. The coroner is reading a book. By describing the dress of the men Bierce suggests that they are mountaineers. The coroner is a man of intelligence. The missing witness enters. He offers as an excuse for his absence the fact that he has been telegraphing to his paper the story of the death. He is obviously from the city. He hastens to add that he has telegraphed the story as fiction, not as fact, for it is unbelievable. The coroner

observes that his testimony must not be mixed
with fiction. The city newspaper man hotly
says that he intends to read his story as testimony, for not only is it as extraordinary as
fiction, it is also truth. He does so. His story
is to the effect that he accepted an invitation
to visit the dead man to enjoy the hunting and
to observe the habits of an educated man who
chose to live in solitude, with a view of incor-
porating him in a story. He finds his friend
strangely distraught but has the good sense
not to ask questions. The next day they prepare to go hunting quail. As they emerge from
the house the visitor notices that the trees at
the edge of the woods are agitated, but the
cause is not visible. He surmises that they have
started a deer. He is astonished to observe that
his friend, an experienced hunter, is staring
with strange intensity in the direction of the
agitated trees. Ironically he asks his friend if
he intends to shoot a deer with shot intended
for quail. His friend does not reply. Suddenly
he observes that the oats that separate the

house from the woods are being bent down as though by a light wind (which he does not feel) with the difference that they do not come up again once the "wind" has passed. There is nothing visible to account for this phenomenon. Suddenly his friend fires in the direction of the invisible force. Then he runs and is suddenly seen to turn and give battle. The struggle is terrific. The arms of the man, thrown out in defence, are blotted out from the watcher's view. The struggler is apparently struggling against nothing. His actions are like those of a man in a fit. The spectator of all this stands petrified. His friend suddenly ceases struggling and falls back to the ground. The spectator then notices that the oats are once more agitated in the odd manner previously described. The agitation continues until it is no longer visible among the trees. Running to his friend the visitor finds him dead. His clothes are torn to shreds, his body bruised and lacerated, his throat torn.

The coroner's jury listens to this. The coroner

exhibits the torn clothing and the mutilated body. The jury render the verdict that the deceased met his death in a struggle with a mountain lion and add that in their opinion he also suffered from fits. The visitor is allowed to go.

Now the obvious explanation for the death of this unfortunate man is that he was murdered. It is equally obvious that the murderer must have been the visitor from the city. It has been emphasized that the jury is loutish, and consequently its judgment of the case is of no importance. On the other hand, the coroner is described as an intelligent man. Since the visitor is a newspaper reporter he may be presumed to be a fairly rational person and not the sort that would expect to have an intelligent coroner believe any obviously cock-and-bull story aimed to exonerate himself of murder. Furthermore, the visitor is so aware of the cock-and-bull nature of his story that he has telegraphed it to his paper as fiction! Yet the coroner accepts the jury's verdict and lets

the young man go without further question.
We have here every available bit of information utilized to substantiate the truth of an
obviously preposterous story. Yet its truth is
subtly suggested to the reader. However, none
of the devices for gaining the reader's assent
to the reality of the situation is overempha-
sized. They are incidental details skilfully
wrought into the story.

The key to the whole situation is an apparently incidental happening. When the young
man returned from telegraphing his story he
noticed that the coroner had been reading, for
he closed a book and put it in his pocket. The
young man also noticed that the book was the
diary of his friend. The inquest over, he asked
for the diary with the idea that it might offer
some clue to the strange death. The coroner
refuses it on the ground that it contains entries made previous to the death and consequently has no relation to the case. But what
he has read in the diary leads him to accept
the apparently cock-and-bull story!

BITTER BIERCE

Some time previous to his death the recluse observed all the phenomena that his friend observed on the day of the strange happening. So fantastic are the phenomena that he believes that he is going insane and decides to invite his friend, as a particularly level-headed chap, to visit him with the notion that he will observe any traces of queerness and take steps to help him regain his balance. Just before his friend's arrival he comes to the conclusion that the invisible menace is a reality and also finds an explanation of its invisibility: "At each end of the solar spectrum the chemist can detect the presence of what are known as 'actinic' rays. They represent colors—integral colors in the composition of light—which we are unable to discern. The human eye is an imperfect instrument; its range is but a few octaves of the real 'chromatic scale.' I am not mad; there are colors that we cannot see. . . . And, God help me! the Damned Thing is of such a color!" The coroner has read this passage before listening to the visitor's testimony which corroborates these conclusions. It disposes him to accept a story which the narrator himself has difficulty in believing and for which he has no rationalization.

But can such things be? Well, *can* they? "The Death of Halpin Frayser." This story, one of the most brilliant that Bierce ever wrote, contains more flash-backs than is usual with him. In outlining it to illuminate, if possible, his technique, I shall not follow them all, but shall bring the story as vividly as possible before the reader's mind with a view to showing how he wove easily explicable happenings into a narrative that reeks of the supernatural.

Halpin Frayser suddenly awoke and uttered the name Catherine Larue. It meant nothing to him. Frayser was sleeping on the ground in the open. He had been out hunting and become lost. Since he thought it useless to wander about in the dark he threw himself down at the foot of a large tree and went to sleep. After uttering this name he once more went off to sleep, but this time he dreamed. He dreamed that he was walking along a road. Suddenly he observed that the puddles were of blood and that blood was splotched over the surrounding trees, bushes, and grass. He tried to find out why he should dream of blood by thinking back over his life in an endeavour to recall some sin he might have committed. He could not. He felt accused and resolved not to submit unheard. He took from his pocket a notebook and started to record his sensations in verse! He was interrupted by the realization that he had heard a hideous laugh and is in the presence of some overpowering force. His dream vision gradually fades out into a vision of his mother in the garments of the grave.

Frayser was a native of Tennessee. He was a dreamy sort of man, a throwback to a type that had but rarely appeared in his practical family. He resembled his grandfather, who had been a poet of sorts. He never attempted poetry, however, but his natural temperament was emphasized by a close attachment to his mother. He was trained at the law. As a young man he had occasion to journey to California (where this story takes place) in the interest of a client. There he was shanghaied and did not get back to San Francisco for six years. He immediately tried to get in touch with his family and was waiting to hear from them when he went hunting.

His sudden disappearance had, of course, worried his mother. She finally came to California to search for her son. She had been widowed and so had an additional interest in finding him. She did not, of course, succeed in doing so. While in California she had married again and her husband, in a fit of mania, had murdered her. He was at large when this story took place. The day following Frayser's strange dream two detectives set out to find the murderer. One of them had developed a theory that the murderer would return to his wife's grave and had resolved to capture him there. Acting on his theory some nights before, he had secreted himself in the cemetery, but he had been caught unawares and overpowered by the murderer, who returned as the detective had figured. Only by good luck had the detective escaped with his life. He was now returning with help to ambush the murderer again. Looking over the ground the two discovered the body of Frayser. He had been murdered. All around him were marks of struggle, and his body showed that he had been strangled. He was lying on the grave of the murdered woman.

Now let us piece together the threads of this strange story. Frayser had been lost. Exhausted he had thrown himself down without too closely observing where he was. By an extraordinary accident he had come to rest in a graveyard. Evidently in a state between sleeping and waking he had read the name of Catherine Larue on the gravestone near which he had thrown himself down without putting two and two together and realizing how strange a resting place he had chosen. When he awoke that name welled up from his subconscious mind to puzzle him. But since he was not of a questioning mind he went to sleep again without thinking deeply of the matter. He dreamed of blood because his mind was naturally occupied with thoughts of his mother, and blood is a sexual symbol. The resolve to exculpate himself from what he took to be an accusation of crime (in reality probably a sense of guilt for his forced neglect of his mother) brought him half awake, and in that state of semi-trance he made his first poetic effort, which was in the manner that subsequent observers noted to be extraordinarily like that of his grandfather. The final apparition of which his mind was conscious was that of his mother. It was in reality the face of the lunatic murderer, who had observed that the figure sitting on the grave was armed and took him to be another detective. So Frayser met his death. By an uncanny accident he had come to sleep on the grave of his mother. Her name by her second marriage was Catherine Larue!

"Moxon's Master." I have chosen this story

for detailed discussion because it seems to me one of the most extraordinary that Bierce ever wrote and because few people have recognized it as such. It seems to me to exhibit his powers functioning on a higher level than was customary with him. It anticipates ideas and situations that have lately been exploited in fiction and on the stage and which have won fame for authors who are not otherwise notable. That Bierce should have undertaken to exploit such modern notions more than thirty years ago illustrates the fact that in many ways he was a forerunner in the field of ideas. "Moxon's Master" is, briefly, a story about a mechanical man who gets out of hand and assumes control over his creator. Emerson deplored the fact that "things are in the saddle, and ride mankind," but Bierce chose to give a specific example of that unfortunate situation. After his fashion he anticipated all those social prophets who are worried about the future of mankind in the machine age.

The story opens with the narrator and

Moxon discussing the possibilities of a machine having the power of thinking. So far as a dictionary definition of a machine goes, man could be called a machine. The crucial point is that a machine is supposed to be a creation of a man and it does not have the power to think. Moxon has become convinced that a machine can think. He points out that plants give evidence of intelligence. He points out that the phenomenon of crystallization is difficult to explain unless one admits an "intelligent coöperation among the constituent elements of the crystals." From that he deduces that machines may be capable of thinking. In fact, he believes that they do so, and his final and clinching point is that "consciousness is the creature of rhythm." A machine works rhythmically and consequently will eventually develop consciousness and finally the power of thought. Moxon develops his thesis with passionate intensity. His friend remains unconvinced.

In his workshop that adjoins the sitting

room in which this conversation had taken place Moxon has a machine that thinks. He has left it running but with nothing to do while he conducts the conversation. Suddenly he excuses himself and enters his workshop. There are sounds of struggle and loud talk. Then all is quiet. Moxon returns with a scratch on his cheek. He says that the machine he has developed has resented his leaving it nothing to do and he has had difficulty in subduing it. The friend is amused and as he leaves takes a parting shot: ". . . I'm going to wish you good-night; and I'll add the hope that the machine which you inadvertently left in action will have her gloves on the next time you think it needful to stop her."

Once out in the rainy night the skeptical visitor finds himself turning over what Moxon had to say. He is partly convinced of the truth of Moxon's position, particularly by the remark "consciousness is the creature of rhythm." He turns back, full of the idea, to discuss it to some reasonable conclusion. He finds the door to Moxon's home open and in his abstraction he does what he has been expressly warned never to do; he opens the door of the laboratory without knocking. An extraordinary sight greets his eyes. He sees Moxon playing chess with an extraordinary being that closely resembles a gorilla. He is struck speechless and watches the performance without stirring or giving the slightest indication that he is there. However, his powers of observation are sufficiently alive for him to notice that Moxon's opponent is a mechanical man! The game goes on without interruption. Moxon plays carelessly, like one extremely distraught. Suddenly he shouts "Check!" gets up quickly, and stands behind his chair.

The automaton sits without moving. The expression on its face does not alter, but suddenly the room is filled with the noise of the mechanism that operates the mechanical man. With terrible suddenness the automaton reaches across the table and grabs Moxon by the throat. There is a struggle, the lights go out, but suddenly there is a blinding flash of flame, and the visitor sees Moxon on the floor, "his throat still in the clutch of those iron hands, his head forced backward, his eyes protruding, his mouth wide open and his tongue thrust out; and—horrible contrast!— upon the painted face of his assassin an expression of tranquil and profound thought, as in the solution of a problem in chess."

The flash of flame sets fire to the building. The visitor is inexplicably rescued by Moxon's assistant. Three days later he recovers consciousness in a hospital. He remembers little of what happened after he saw Moxon in the grip of the mechanical man. But that is impressed upon his mind. A machine murdered its maker!

Now in this story Bierce has used *ideas* to heighten his effect. He carefully manipulates the whole situation so that the logic of what is said leads inevitably to the conclusion that a machine *may* develop the power of thought. By having Moxon's interlocutor maintain an

179

attitude of skepticism he provides an antidote against the reader's skepticism. By insisting upon one idea, that "consciousness is the creature of rhythm," he distracts attention from some of the more obvious objections to the idea that a machine may become sentient. It is this idea that convinces the skeptical visitor. With a view of increasing the unreality of the situation, Bierce introduces a quite commonplace device; he has the whole affair take place during a thunderstorm. Returning to Moxon's house in a half-convinced state the visitor is mentally prepared to believe. He sees the automaton in action. His doubts are dissipated. Bierce consequently rushes his story to its conclusion. Such an unnatural thing as a machine that can think cannot continue to exist in the world. It kills its maker. Fire destroys every trace of its existence. Its reality rests on the testimony of a man who was mentally prepared for belief by a prolonged argument and whose memories of actually having seen a mechanical man in action that presupposes thought are shaken by a personal catastrophe that led to three days' unconsciousness. The reader is therefore free to remain in the same state of mind as when he began the story. He need not be convinced. He is almost forced, however, to debate the question, "Can such things be?"

These four stories represent Bierce handling four different ideas, all of which have something to do with the supernatural. They are unusual happenings that have impinged on the normal tenor of events. It will have been observed that Bierce never demanded that the reader approach his stories with a "will to believe." He saw to it that within the story itself were incorporated all the facts and sidelights necessary to lead into a state of mind that would minimize skepticism. The effects he achieved, then, are the product of a careful mixture of the facts of ordinary life with the supernatural. Neither one is allowed to dominate. It is difficult to tell where one leaves off and the other begins. That Bierce himself did not know seems to me logical to suppose.

It has been suggested to me that there must have been some obscure psychological reason for Bierce's interest in the horrible. I do not think so. It may well be that there was a twist in Bierce's mind that led him to deal with such matters with particular pleasure, but my point is that I do not think we need be worried if we cannot isolate it. It seems to me that his interest is clearly and adequately explained as a natural extension of his literary ideas that I outlined in an earlier chapter.

Neither does it seem to me that there is much importance in the familiar remark that it is nerve-racking to read his stories. Bierce himself, apropos his war stories, remarked: "If it scares you to read that one imaginary character killed another imaginary character, why not take up knitting instead of reading?" It may, however, be noted that it is extremely unfortunate that Bierce did not treat other than "nerve-racking" subjects. He certainly had all the literary skill necessary for widening his range of topics. If he had, his books would have been more balanced and the possibility that his effects would become tedious by repetition would have been avoided. It is unfortunate that Bierce never ran across the remark of Sir Walter Scott that Lafcadio Hearn quoted in the preface to *Some Chinese Ghosts:* "The supernatural, though appealing to certain powerful emotions very widely and deeply sown amongst the human race, is, nevertheless, a spring which is peculiarly apt to lose its elasticity by being too much pressed upon."

Chapter 4

ON SATIRE AND WIT

"FOR ALL our professed delight in and capacity for jocosity, we have produced so far but one genuine wit—Ambrose Bierce—and, save to a small circle, he remains unknown to-day." These words are H. L. Mencken's, and they have been quoted in season and out by Bierce's fanatical partisans. On the other side of the argument is Gilbert Seldes, who wrote of Bierce: ". . . Certainly he had intelligence and wrote respectable English with a cold pen. His *Dictionary* does not impress me as the work of a spirit naturally ironical." Between these two opinions there must be a middle ground, and that is the position that will be taken in this brief discussion of Bierce as satirist and wit. For a close study of Bierce's work reveals the fact that a good deal of his

184

satire is dull and almost unreadable to-day. It has lost its relevancy because it was directed against temporary situations. Bierce's satire as a rule was not directed against permanent foibles of the human race. In the same way a good deal of his wit was aimed to annihilate persons of such slight importance that they cannot be identified now by the moderately well-informed reader. Nevertheless, it is possible to make out a better case for his wit than for his satire. The latter had better be left to moulder undisturbed.

Examples of his wit have been scattered freely throughout this book, and if the reader has not appreciated these he is not likely to be convinced of Bierce's wittiness by anything that can be said here. Wit is a difficult thing to write about.[1] It must be quoted so that it

---

[1]Mr. Wilson Follette published an essay in the *Bookman* for November, 1928, in which he gave a brilliant analysis of Bierce's wit— a verbal analysis. He makes what in my opinion are extravagant claims for the merit of Bierce's fables, even more extravagant claims for the value of Bierce's verse, and underestimates the value of the fiction, but my disagreement as to these matters does not blind me to the worth of the essay as a whole.

may be savoured. Bierce had very definite notions about wit. "Wit," he wrote, "may make us smile, or make us wince, but laughter —that is the cheaper price that we pay for an inferior entertainment, namely, humor. . . . Humor is Artemus Ward, John Phoenix, Josh Billings, Petroleum V. Nasby, Bill Nye, Mark Twain,—their name is legion; for wit we must brave the perils of the deep: It is 'made in France' and hardly bears transportation. Nearly all Americans are humorous; if any are born witty, Heaven help them to emigrate." Wit he defined as something not altogether true, so not dull; it has enough audacity to startle; enough paradox to charm; it must be profoundly wise and bleak as steel. If we test his own wit by these criteria we shall find that he did not fall much below the standards he set.

Unfortunately, he had one fault that takes the edge off some of his wit. He was not satisfied to startle by paradox, to be wise and bleak; he thought it necessary to score a knock-out every time he took up his pen. His wit is of the knockdown variety. Perhaps he underestimated the capacity of the Americans to "get" his wit and overwrote in an effort to make his point obvious. The examples that have been cited will illustrate the truth or untruth of this criticism. As a substitute for probably aimless writing about a thing so evanescent as wit I shall assemble a few more examples here. Since wit is a matter of taste, those who are familiar with Bierce's wit, or who are moved to become so as a result of this monograph, may object that I have chosen the wrong examples. However . . .

Speaking of the writers who produce a novel a year he wrote: "The amount of patient research, profound thought and systematic planning that go to the making of one of their books is (naturally) astonishing. Unfortunately it falls just short of the amount that kills."

*   *   *

"Christians and camels receive their burdens kneeling."

"A connoisseur is a specialist who knows everything about something and nothing about anything else."

*   *   *

"Impunity. Wealth."

*   *   *

"To kill is to create a vacancy without nominating a successor."

*   *   *

"Learning is the kind of ignorance distinguishing the studious."

*   *   *

"To be positive is to be mistaken at the top of one's voice."

*   *   *

"A prejudice is a vagrant opinion without visible means of support."

*   *   *

"A saint is a dead sinner revised and edited."

*   *   *

"The senate is a body of elderly gentlemen charged with high duties and misdemeanors."

BITTER BIERCE

"To be truthful is to be dumb and illiterate."

*   *   *

"Is it because Christ is an unknown quantity that Christians write: Xmas?"

Chapter 5

POETRY

As a poet, Bierce was a failure. His hostility to emotional utterance was an impenetrable barrier to his success in poetry. He had some sense of rhetoric, but it was conventional rhetoric. Indeed, I am unable to find any redeeming qualities of importance even in those of his poems that George Sterling chose as Bierce's best. They all strike me as pretty trivial, and the two bulky volumes that contain them are the least important of the many unimportant volumes in his *Collected Works*. That he had misgivings about the wisdom of reprinting his poetry may be seen by the defensive remarks he made in the prefaces to the volumes: "To one having only a reader's interest in the matter it may seem that the verses relating to those person's censored might prop-

erly have been omitted from this collection."
Indeed they might, for the bulk of the censori-
ous verses are quite impossible to read with
anything like interest. Of the entire volume,
Black Beetles in Amber, he wrote: "Most of the
verses in this volume are republished from
newspapers and periodicals of the Pacific
Coast. Naturally, the collection includes few
not relating to persons and events more or less
familiar to the people of that interesting
region—to whom, indeed, the volume may be
considered as especially addressed, though not
without a hope that its contents may be found
to have a sufficient intrinsic interest to commend it to others." There is less to "commend
it to others" to-day than there was fourteen
years ago. The most interesting part of Bierce's
poetry is the titles he chose for his volumes:
Black Beetles in Amber and *Shapes of Clay*.

Fortunately he did not think much of himself as a poet. He wrote (this passage is col-
lated from several letters): "I am not a poet,
but an abuser—that makes all the difference

... so I'm entitled to credit for what little gold there may be in the mud I throw. But if I professed gold-throwing, the mud which I should surely mix with the missiles would count against me. ... When old Homer, Shakespeare and that crowd—building better than Ozymandias—say: 'Look on my works ye mighty, and despair!' I, considering myself specially addressed, despair."

For the benefit of the curious it may be mentioned that George Sterling selected the following poems by Bierce as his best: "Invocation," "Reminded," "Another Way," "Death of Grant" (strangely enough a eulogy unqualified), "Presentment," "T. A. H.," and "Geotheos." It is not my intention to inflict any one of these poems upon the reader. They will hardly bear quotation. A typical stanza (from "Geotheos") may be cited, however:

> As sweet as the look of a lover
> Saluting the eyes of a maid
> That blossom to blue as the maid

BITTER BIERCE

Is ablush to the glances above her,
The sunshine is gilding the glade
And lifting the lark out of shade

Something might be made of Bierce as a writer of *vers de société*. There are some examples of his work in this field that I can imagine appearing in F. P. A.'s column any morning. (F. P. A. will please verify this assumption.) To cite an example or two:

NOT GUILTY

"I saw your charms in another's arms,"
  Said a Grecian swain with his blood a-boil;
"And he kissed you fair as he held you there,
  A willing bird in a serpent's coil."

The maid looked up from the cinctured cup
  Wherein she was crushing the berries red,
Pain and surprise in her honest eyes—
  "It was only one o' those gods," she said.

DISCRETION

She:

  I'm told that men have sometimes got
  Too confidential, and

Have said to one another what
  They—well, you understand.
I hope I don't offend you, sweet,
  But are you sure that you're discreet?

He:

'Tis true, sometimes my friends in wine
  Their conquests do recall,
But none can truly say that mine
  Are known to him at all.
I never, never talk you o'er—
In truth, I never get the floor.

But I imagine that these verses will strike the reader as highly incongruous when compared to Bierce's other work.

More typical of him are his invectives in verse. Some of them still have interest to-day, for they were directed against persons still fresh in the public mind. The one dealing with Carnegie is particularly interesting:

AN IMPOSTOR

Must you, Carnegie, evermore explain
Your worth, and all the reasons give again
Why black and red are similarly white
And you and God identically right?

BITTER BIERCE

Still must our ears without redress submit
To hear you play the solemn hypocrite
Walking in spirit some high moral level,
Raising at once his eyeballs and the devil?
Great King of Cant! if Nature had but made
Your mouth without a tongue I ne'er had prayed
To have an earless head. Since she did not,
Bear me, ye whirlwinds, to some favored spot—
Some mountain pinnacle that sleeps in air
So delicately, mercifully rare
That when the fellow climbs the giddy hill,
As, for my sins, I know at last he will,
To utter twaddle in that void inane
His soundless organ he will play in vain.

So, too, we may find it interesting to cite
one example of Bierce's ante-mortem epitaphs:

A TRENCHER–KNIGHT

Stranger, uncover; here you have in view
The monument of Chauncey M. Depew,
Eater and orator, the whole world round
In feats of tongue and tooth alike renowned.
Dining his way to eminence, he rowed
With knife and fork up water-ways that flowed
From lakes of favor—pulled with all his force
And found each river sweeter than the source.

195

BITTER BIERCE

Like rats, obscure beneath a kitchen floor,
Gnawing and rising till obscure no more,
He ate his way to eminence, and Fame
Inscribes in gravy his immortal name.

A trencher-knight, he, mounted on his belly,
So spurred his charger that its sides were jelly.
Grown desperate at last, it reared and threw him,
And indigestion, overtaking, slew him.

For the rest silence is the wisest policy.

PART III
IDEAS

Chapter 1

LIFE IN GENERAL

IN THE life of man Bierce found little that was inspiring. His findings can be phrased thus: Man commands no respect, nor does woman: "an animal usually living in the vicinity of man, and having a rudimentary susceptibility to domestication." Her bait for man is beauty. United in marriage, the only cure for that temporary insanity, love, man and woman become slaves the one of the other. They live in a house: "A hollow edifice erected for the habitation of man, rat, mouse, beetle, cockroach, fly, mosquito, flea, bacillus and microbe." One boon they can confer upon another animal, childhood: "The period of human life intermediate between the idiocy of infancy and the folly of youth—two removes from the sin of manhood and three

from the remorse of age." But even that boon
has to be prefaced by a disgusting episode,
infancy: "The period of our lives when, according to Wordsworth, 'Heaven lies about
us.' The world begins lying about us pretty
soon afterward." That brief period between
infancy and youth was all of life that Bierce
discovered to be undefiled. With methodical
persistence he proceeded from a day, "a period
of twenty-four hours, mostly misspent," to
the year, "a period of three hundred and sixty-
five disappointments." Launched on life dominated by such a calendar, the human animal
can expect little—and gets it. To be sure, he
has small equipment to rise superior to the ills
that flesh is heir to. His head contains about as
much brain as a cabbage. His heart is simply
"an automatic, muscular bloodpump." The
emotions and sentiments are generated in the
stomach "being evolved from food by chemical
action of the gastric fluid." His principal
motivating force is fear. In fact, he cannot
even be sure that he is, for Descartes' famous

epigram should really read, according to Bierce, *Cogito cogito ergo cogito sum.*

The reigning dynasty in life and letters is the Dullards. Ability is largely useless, but supposing one is so unfortunate as to be endowed with it, it will be found to consist mostly of solemnity. Ambition, also a handicap, is an "overmastering desire to be vilified by enemies while living and made ridiculous by friends when dead." And if ambition should lead to achievement nothing much is accomplished, for achievement is simply "the death of endeavor and the birth of disgust." Any congratulations one may collect are motivated by envy.

It is the height of folly to distinguish one's self in any way from the masses of men, for any deviation from the ordinary is abnormal, and to be abnormal is to be detested. Too great intellectual independence is "madness." The best course is conformity. Expect nothing of others. Put aside romantic notions of friendship—a fair-weather device only. Be sure that in adversity you will be privileged to contem-

plate your "friend's" back. Contemplating
those in adversity when one is safe from harm
is productive of the greatest happiness in
man. All beggars are those who have "relied
on the assistance of friends." Beware of
kindness anyhow, for it is a "brief preface to
ten volumes of exaction."

Be not misled into believing that your thinking is disinterested. Deliberation is merely
"the act of examining one's bread to determine which side it is buttered on." When
you are impartial you merely are unable to
discover personal advantage "from espousing
either side of a controversy or adopting either
of two conflicting opinions." It is advantage-
ous to be as hypocritical as possible, for then
one "secures the advantage of seeming to be
what one despises."

The end of life is the pursuit of pleasure, but
one who overtakes pleasure is a debauchee.
That is immoral which is inexpedient, and
that is inexpedient which is not "calculated
to advance one's interest." It varies with cir-

cumstances. To act always with impunity one must be wealthy—and the measure of your respectability is your income. Wealth also allows one to cultivate a repose of manner that in the poor is called laziness.

The most acceptable end of life is failure, for success is "the one unpardonable sin against one's fellows." So, too, should life be short, even if not merry, for longevity is merely an "uncommon extension of the fear of death." And so in the end one is drawn out to the cemetery in a hearse ("death's baby carriage") and deposited in a grave:

> Done with the work of breathing; done
> With all the world; the mad race run
> Through to the end; the golden goal
> Attained and found to be a hole!

In this sketch woman is considered chiefly in relation to man. Taken by herself she suffers, in addition to all the ills that man contends with, the additional handicaps of mental and social inferiority. Bierce was a fierce anti-feminist. He opposed woman suffrage as well as all attempts by women to enter the professions and business. In dead earnest he wrote: "The 'enlargement of woman's opportunities' has benefited individual women. It has not benefited the sex as a whole, and has distinctly damaged the race. The mind that cannot discern a score of great and irreparable general evils distinctly traceable to 'emancipation of woman' is as impregnable to the light as a toad in a rock." In a letter he wrote succinctly his opinion of a specific woman's brains. He was not joking entirely. "That girl has a bushel of brains, and her father and brother have to look out for her or she will leave them out of sight. I would suggest as a measure of precaution against so monstrous a perversion of natural order that she have her eyes put out. The subjection of women must be maintained." Indeed, Bierce was one of the very few American men who refused to bow to the tyranny of American women, which is a phenomenon that is noted with astonishment by all foreign observers. He granted them charm and beauty and urged them to cultivate both, but to his mind women of brains were unnatural phenomena. He told them that "there is one service of incomparable utility and dignity for which I esteem you eminently fit—to be mothers of men."

As usual, there is an excess of bitterness in Bierce's summary of life and of the capacities of the human animal. Bierce found more in life than he cared to acknowledge. Up until his last years, when his personal life became flat and empty, he had a good time. The barren end was the result of a crucial weakness in his life, peculiar to so many men whose philosophy is bitter. Bierce failed to find anything that would serve as a buttress against the pressure of life; he failed to develop an interest in anything that would serve as a refuge when the world palled. No matter how completely one may destroy one's belief in conventional sops, unless one does find something, spiritual death is inevitable. Terror and horror at the emptiness of their lives have driven men of vast critical capacity into the Catholic Church whose essence is unquestioning belief. Bierce's only escape was a return to a life of action. His interior resources were nil. His culture was so limited and he took so little interest in expanding it that he could not take refuge in it when he felt himself played out. It seems beyond question that the happiest period of his life was the Civil War days. (This may be compared with Mark Twain's supremely happy period, the Mississippi River days when he was a pilot.) Consequently, Bierce ended his life in the handiest situation comparable to the Civil War, the Mexican Revolution.

Labouring under no illusions about life he found satisfaction in the most conventional of human values (most of them discussed earlier), friendship with both men and women, particularly the latter, presumably not emancipated, sport, eating, and drinking. He had a good time in personal journalism and enjoyed nothing so much as swatting frauds and crooks. He took pleasure in the writing of his stories, but that composition was a source of permanent satisfaction with him I presume to doubt. There is no discoverable evidence that it played the same sustaining part in his life that it played in Flaubert's, say. His philosophy of life was such that had he been able to find some permanent interest he would have lived happily enough to a serene old age. He believed it the better part of discretion to conform one's *conduct* to the prevailing notions of what was right and confine one's rebelliousness to the intellectual sphere.

His relations with his fellow men, though friendship was a fetish with him, were not the happiest, as has been pointed out. He aimed to carry his convictions into his conduct, and the results were disastrous. Once again his dogmatism tended to destroy whatever merits his ideas may have had. Nowhere is it necessary to give more place to mutations from fixed rules than in human relationships.

Joseph Lewis French called Bierce an old Presbyterian, and others have been equally severe. Such judgments are unjust. Bierce had high enough notions about conduct, and was severe enough in applying them, but at least in his old age he was far more tolerant than an old Presbyterian. On the sexual morality of his friends he once wrote that he did not think it wise to be exacting. Of himself he noted: "I would not take another man's woman, any more than I would take his purse. Nor, I trust, would I seduce the daughter or sister of a friend, nor any maid whom it would at all damage—and as to *that* there is no hard and fast rule."

Bierce made one suggestion as to how to improve the human race that even to-day is looked at askance by all but the most advanced thinkers. He believed that the application of the principles of selective breeding to human beings would be decidedly for the good of society. Since it is only a step from this to

steriiization of the unfit, I think we may assume that he would have supported this measure had he known about it. He wrote: "As to
stirpiculture, the intelligent and systematic
breeding of men and women with a view to
improvement of the species—it is a thing of
the far future. It is hardly in sight. Yet, what
splendid possibilities it carries! Two or three
generations of as careful breeding as we bestow
on horses, dogs and pigeons would do more
good than all the penal, reformatory and
educating agencies of the world accomplish in
a thousand years. It is the one direction in
which human effort to 'elevate the race' can
be assured of a definitive, speedy and adequate
success. It is hardly better than nonsense to
prate of any good coming to the race through
(for example) medical science, which is mainly
concerned in reversing the beneficent opera-
tion of natural laws and saving the inefficient
to perpetuate their inefficiency. Our entire
system of charities is open to the same objection; it preserves the incapables whom Nature

is trying to 'weed out.' This not only debases the race physically, intellectually and morally, but constantly increases the rate of debasement. The proportion of criminals, paupers and the several kinds of 'inmates' augments its horrible percentage yearly. On the other hand, our wars destroy the capable; so thus we make inroads upon the vitality of the race from two directions. We preserve the feeble and extirpate the strong. He who in view of this amazing folly can believe in a constant, even slow, progress of the human race toward perfection ought to be happy. He has a mind whose Olympian heights are inaccessible—the Titans of fact can never scale them to storm its ancient, solitary reign."

It was with these ideas in mind that he advocated harsh prison discipline and the death penalty. Beyond doubt he was wrong in his belief that severity of punishment is a deterrent of crime, but what he was after was right. He sought to eliminate the criminal element from society. He wanted to confine them permanently to prison as modern penologists advocate the permanent segregation of congenital criminals and especially recidivists. As to the death penalty all he sought was to eliminate at one stroke a member of society who had given positive evidence of homicidal traits. To be sure he did think that execution might deter others from homicide but that was to be incidental. Like modern criminologists, furthermore, he did not propose to wait until a person of homicidal traits had committed murder before eliminating him from society. He wrote: "The scientist who will tell us how to recognize the potential assassin, and persuade us to kill him, will be the greatest benefactor of his century." And finally, with characteristic Biercean logicality, he imagined that if all those dangerous to society who were not executed were confined to prisons, that the problem of the guards would not be to keep their charges in, but to keep the few individuals left at large from breaking in to enjoy some company of human kind!

BITTER BIERCE

A correlation of Bierce's ideas about conduct
and of his ideas about a desirable world to live
in should give one some comprehension of his
notion of the good life. "The purpose of every
sane human being," he wrote, "is to be happy."
Bierce imagined a good life ruled by the highest standards of personal and social honour.
He believed firmly in doing unto others what
you would have others do unto you. Both of
these fundamental ideas would have played a
part in determining his code of sexual morality.
It would have been severe but not conventional. He never formulated it. Religion and
other superstitions he proposed to abolish. He
would have demanded that the productive
and distributive aspects of economy be reduced to the service of the community while
yet remaining strictly capitalistic in organization. He would have reorganized politics on an
aristocratic basis. Cultural concerns would
assume a paramount place in the lives of the
aristocracy. Eating and drinking he would
have erected into arts. Mankind in general

would be so handled as to be tolerable. Bierce asked nothing more.

It is strange in what extraordinary contrast stand Bierce's notions of the life of man in his day, his own life, and his conception of the good life. But does not the conflict between the first and last explain his own defeat?

Chapter 2

ECONOMICS

ALTHOUGH Bierce recognized that a good many of the ills of society were the product of economic forces, he nevertheless did not regard them as inherent in the capitalistic system. Like H. L. Mencken to-day, he believed that a change in the directing personnel would make capitalism a completely satisfactory economy. Rather than regarding the crooks and bounders as inevitable products of the system, he attributed the weaknesses and worse to the crooks and bounders. This is part and parcel of his fundamental idea that heredity, in the last analysis, was more important than environment. To my way of thinking he was wrong in making heredity and environment warring concepts. They are rather complementing factors.

Of course Bierce did not have an acute sense of the recent origin and rapid evolution of capitalist economy. Though he made a great parade of viewing things historically, his writings do not indicate that he knew much about the past. Bierce's use of history was in the other direction; he delighted in projecting his imagination into the future and predicting all sorts of dire happenings if present trends continued.

Contemporary commerce Bierce identified with piracy. To him it was an organized skin game. No dodge was so low that a business man would not use it. As remarked earlier, he conceived an ideal commonwealth where commerce would be a means of equitably distributing goods. He saw no evidence in his own day that such a motive ever entered into business. As to production, he wanted to avoid crass exploitation and unemployment. While yet keeping the lower orders down, I imagine that he aimed at a sort of paternal capitalism, permeated with a somewhat feudalistic relation between employers and employed. A bitter critic of social conditions himself, he could not tolerate critiques that found in the evils evidence that the system was fundamentally wrong. He himself attacked both employers and employees. Neither held, or was moving toward, his ideals.[1] He would have found more to-day to his taste. For more reasons than one I can imagine him admiring Henry Ford.

Bierce was severe on deliberate exploitation of employees or the general public and especially so on the hypocritically moral attitude of those who practised exploitation. His opposition to Collis Huntington is a case in point. He was also severe on Andrew Carnegie, whom he called a "smugwump." On the morals of exploitation he wrote as follows: "Human nature is pretty well balanced; for

---

[1]Apropos the Homestead strike he wrote in a letter: "I have no sympathies with that savage fight between the two kinds of rascals, and no desire to assist either—except to better hearts and manners. The love of truth is good enough motive for me when I write of my fellow men. I like many things in this world and a few persons—I like you for example; but after they are served I have no love to waste upon the irreclaimable mass of brutality that we know as 'mankind.' Compassion, yes—I am sincerely sorry that they are brutes."

every lacking virtue there is a rough substitute that will serve at a pinch—as cunning is the wisdom of the unwise, and ferocity the courage of the coward. Nobody is altogether bad; the scoundrel who has grown rich by underpaying workmen in his factory will sometimes endow an asylum for indigent seamen. To oppress one's own workmen, and provide for the workmen of a neighbor—to skin those in charge of one's own interests while cottoning and oiling the residuary product of another's skinnery— that is not very good benevolence, nor very good sense, but it serves in place of both. The man who eats *pâté de foie gras* in the sweat of his girl cashier's face, or wears purple and fine linen in order that his typewriter may have an eocene gown and a pliocene hat, seems a tolerably satisfactory specimen of the genus thief; but let us not forget that in his own home—a fairly good one—he may enjoy and merit that highest and most honorable title on the scroll of woman's favor, 'a good provider.' One having claim to that glittering distinction should enjoy immunity from the coarse and troublesome question, 'From whose backs and bellies do you provide?'" This is in line with Harry Elmer Barnes's oft-reiterated remark that it is conventionally moral in our present society deliberately to wreck a corporation but immoral to kiss one's stenographer.

The other aspect of modern capitalism that deeply offended his sense of decency was the existence of unemployment. He said bluntly enough: "So unfortunate and dangerous a creature as a man able and willing to work, yet having no work to do, should be unknown outside the literature of satire. . . . The right to employment being the right to life, its denial is, in a sense, homicide." It is sad to think, he observed, that in the highest "state of civilization nine-tenths of mankind have to struggle in the lowest battle of savage or even animal man—the battle against famine."

But the essence of Bierce's criticism of the economy he knew was that it was conducted in a way of which no honourable man could approve. This is also the essence of Mencken's criticism and Van Wyck Brooks is only one among many to point out that Mencken has propounded many of Bierce's ideas with less finesse and more learning.

Bierce's understanding of capitalism made him a defender of trusts when "trust busting" was the order of the day. He saw clearly enough that with commercial morals what they were, a trust would simply aggravate a bad condition, but he saw that trusts could, when properly regulated, contribute a vast amount to the public weal. He therefore advocated regulation and not destruction. In vast combinations of capital, administered by honourable men with no use for predatory policies, he saw a desirable organization for industry. The benefits to be expected were reduced costs in production and distribution, steadier employment, better opportunities for workmen, an improved product, and a lower price.

Unfortunately, as he also saw, there was little prospect of realizing this without a complete change in what he called human nature, an inherent element in which was selfishness. He did have a remedy, but I cannot convince myself that he was not joking when he proposed it. Anyhow, he knew it wouldn't be accepted. More of this shortly. Consequently, he imagined that before anything could be arranged the whole of civilization would be brought low by an alliance between capital and labour—two selfishnesses combined to war upon the general public. Bierce hated labour unions and labour leaders worse than poison. He was as vehement against them as any large employer of labour of his day. He did not recognize that lowered costs and larger output per unit might warrant higher wages and shorter hours than those of the day. That aspect of the benefits accruing from trusts did not occur to him. Consequently he regarded labour as a rankly exploitive group—worse if anything than the predatory capitalists. An alliance of labour and capital was, therefore, his idea of the most disastrous thing that could happen to society. This combination would eventually bring things to such a pass that the public would openly rebel. The total collapse of American civilization would result. He projected this disaster thus: "A man in St. Louis purchased a sheep's kidney for seven-and-a-half dollars. In his rage at the price he exclaimed: 'As a public man I have given twenty of the best years of my life bringing about a friendly understanding between capital and labour. I have succeeded, and may God have mercy on my meddlesome soul!' The remark was resented, a riot ensued and when the sun went down that evening his last beams fell upon a city reeking with the blood of a hundred millionaires and twenty thousand citizens and sons of toil. Students of the history of those troublous times need not to be told other and more awful events followed that bloody reprisal. Within forty-eight hours the country was ablaze with insurrection, followed by intestinal wars which lasted three hundred and seventy years and were marked by such hideous barbarities as the modern historian can hardly bring himself to relate. The entire stupendous edifice of popular government, temple and citadel of fallacies and abuses, had crashed to ruin. For centuries its fallen columns and scattered stones sheltered an ever diminishing number of skulking anarchists, succeeded by hordes of skin-clad savages subsisting on offal and raw flesh— the remnant of an extinct civilization. And finally all vanished from history into a darkness impenetrable to conjecture."

In spite of his enmity to them, Bierce, undoubtedly while laughing up his sleeve, proposed to reconcile the two groups and dissolve all their differences by an application of Jesus' injunction: "Whatsoever ye would that men should do unto you, even so do ye also unto them." He imagined a crowd gathered on the steps of the Capitol at Washington, attracted by an advertisement to the effect that a prophet would tell how to solve the industrial impasse. ". . . A tall, pale man clad in a long robe, bareheaded, his hair falling lightly upon his shoulders, his eyes full of compassion, and with such majesty of face and mien that all were awed to silence ere he spoke. Stepping slowly forward toward the throng and raising his right hand from its elbow, the index finger extended upward, he said, in a voice ineffably sweet and serious: 'Whatsoever ye would that men should do unto you, even so do ye also unto them.'" This astonishing pronouncement produced a riot in which the dominant cry was "Lynch him!" but "Crucify him!" was also heard. That he should have bothered himself to advocate the application of the Golden Rule to industrial relations is most amusing, for his hatred of reformers was quite vicious.

For some reason I have not been able to fathom, Bierce made an attack on one of the roots of capitalism; he attacked private property in land and particularly natural resources. This is certainly entirely out of harmony with his fundamental notions and was, perhaps, a result of his sense of the ridiculous. It struck him as very funny that any man born into the world could only live, move, and have his being on sufferance. Unless he had the good luck to acquire property in land, he would all his life be a trespasser on the property of others. Truly, he remarked, man in this world very frequently has no place where he can lay his head and call it his own. He also wrote caustic criticisms of insurance—life and fire, Grand Army pensions (his own of thirty dollars a month he called "cigar money"), and protection. In spite of these aberrations, Bierce was an old-fashioned man who believed that if the world would adopt his ideals of honour and uprightness all would be well.

His enmity to democracy led him to attack such social movements as aimed further to hamper the already emasculated aristocratic elements in society. Socialism and anarchism seemed to him to be stages on the road to ruin. Socialists and socialism aroused his worst passions. In few matters did he do such

224

sloppy and inconsequential thinking as in his diatribes against the socialists. Though he did recognize that socialism was the apotheosis of government and anarchism its negation, he usually lumped the two together and argued that the socialist was merely paving the way for the anarchist. As an alarmist Bierce worked on the level of the radical-baiters of to-day. The Russian Revolution would have made him hysterical.

It is quite obvious that Bierce never put his thoughts about economy into order. He left a great many questions up in the air, but we can identify an undercurrent in his writings in this field which was brought out into the open when he discussed politics. Bierce had in mind an aristocratic society based on a highly sublimated capitalism.

Chapter 3

POLITICS

IT IS not so difficult to systematize Bierce's ideas on politics as it was to arrange those on economics. He went into the matter more thoroughly because it was a more permanent concern of his. Nevertheless, he left his thoughts incomplete because he did not have an audience for them. There was nothing to stimulate him logically to arrange his ideas.

Bierce belongs in the anti-democratic tradition in American political thought that goes back to Alexander Hamilton and John Adams and numbers among its adherents outstanding publicists as different as Ralph Waldo Emerson and H. L. Mencken. Like all of his social ideas his anti-democratic political attitude was rooted in his contempt for the masses. In this also he was at one with Adams, Hamilton,

BITTER BIERCE

Emerson, and Mencken. "My allegiance to republican institutions is slack," he wrote, "through lack of faith in them as a practical system of governing men as men are." What he thought of men we have already noted. Nevertheless, he was not a monarchist. "I will call no man 'your majesty,' nor 'your lordship.' For me to meet in my own country a king or a nobleman would require as much preliminary negotiation as an official interview between the Mufti of Moosh and the Ahkoond of Swat. The form of salutation and the style and title of address would have to be settled definitely and with precision." Bierce favoured government by an aristocracy of brains—not by an hereditary aristocracy. He was not a Nietzschean either. I doubt that he ever heard of Nietzsche, much less read him. Morally he was pre-Nietzschean, but I think we may borrow Georg Brandes's term for Nietzsche and call Bierce an "aristocratic radical."

Starting from his enormous contempt for

the common man, Bierce elaborated a political system the like of which no one else in his day even vaguely imagined. But first let us note his criticism of democracy. Already we have seen that he emphasized a social result of democracy, insistence on conformity, and of course he recognized its significance in politics. The necessity for government arises out of man's inherent folly and badness. Its purpose is to bring order out of anarchy. Therefore, to be efficacious it should be imposed on man from above by those of the populace possessed of brains and a high sense of honour. Democracy is theoretically based on the will of the masses, or men of notorious folly and badness attempt to say how they shall be governed! The idea is, further, that while admitting that individually man is usually incapable of solving any of the intricate problems of modern government, by some occult process he is capable collectively. Though he does not know how to attack the problems himself, he can choose a man who is capable. This is palpable nonsense, for folly added to folly never made sense. Public opinion, far from being the highest common denominator in political wisdom, is usually the lowest. Politicians, being persons whose sole purpose is to hold office, flatter the mob in its idiocies. In the United States there are two major parties, ostensibly opposed, but actually indistinguishable in aims and ideas. Political struggles are not conflicts of principles but conflicts of interests, and the chief object is to get office and carry off as much swag as possible. The opposition party in the government is useful only in that it keeps the administration from getting away with too much swag. It desires that some be left when it gains control. Yet Bierce, after years of observation in Washington, concluded that: "There are no Cæsars of crime, but about a dozen rascals, all told, mostly very small fellows; I can name them all. They are without power or influence enough to count in the scheme of legislation. The really dangerous

chaps are the demagogues, the friends of the
peepul. And they do the 'shouting.' Compared
with the Congress of our forefathers, the Congress of to-day is a flock of angels to an execu-
tive body of the Western Federation of Min-
ers." In a way Bierce anticipated what is now
a reality—the ascendency of "pressure" groups
in dictating governmental policies.

Naturally, Bierce had a good deal to say
about graft at one time and another, but nothing he said has the satirical point of this
observation on the pork-barrel system. He
had travelled to the Island of Ug in the Land
Beyond the Blow: "I was once greatly amused
by a spirited contest over a matter of harbor
improvement, each of the two harbors having
its advocates. One of the gentlemen, a most
eloquent patriot, held the floor for hours in
advocacy of the port where he had an interest
in a projected mill for making dead kittens
into cauliflower pickles; while the other members were being vigorously persuaded by one
who at the other place had a clam ranch."

Any extensions of democracy, in politics as in economics, of course, aroused his bitterest animosity. In November, 1911, he wrote to George Sterling: "I note that at the late election California damned herself to a still lower degradation and is now unfit for a white man to live in. Initiative, referendum, recall, employers' liability, woman suffrage—yah!"

Looking back over what he knew of history Bierce found that there was no type of government that had been a success. The trouble was that no matter how desirable the head of the government may have been, it was impossible to find able and upright men to carry on the administration. "Under any conceivable system the cleverest, most enterprising and least scrupulous men will be at the head of affairs, and they will not be there 'for their health.'" Nevertheless, he held it axiomatic that the essence of government was the restraint of the many by the few—"the subordination of numbers to brains." Such a programme means: ". . . the denial to the masses of the

231

right to cut their own throats and ours. It means grasp and control of all social forces and material energy—a vigilant censorship of the press, a firm hand upon the churches, keen supervision of public meetings and public amusements, command of the railroads, telegraphs and all means of communication. It means, in short, ability to make use of all beneficent influences of enlightenment for the general good, and to array all the powers of civilization against civilization's natural enemies—'the masses.' Government like this has a thousand defects, but it has one merit: it is a government. Despotism? Yes. It is the despotisms of the world that have been the conservators of civilization.''

Bierce, then, imagined the best government to be a despotism of brains. Its purpose was to save civilization from the mob. His misgivings about democracy were all formulated before the Great War—a good while before—and may sound stale now, when "democratic misgivings" have become the platitudes of the intellectuals. But how are we to treat his prophecy that his type of despotism will naturally grow out of democracy once the latter has sunk into an anarchy no longer tolerable to men of culture? And how are we to treat his contention that only under despotism can culture survive? To-day we have despotisms in Russia, Italy, and Spain. Are they steps in the direction of a higher culture?

Of all the recent books of a political tendency that I have read none seems to me more in harmony with Bierce's ideas than Clive Bell's *Civilization*. On the possibility that despotism may be the best setting for a higher culture than we now have, Mr. Bell says: "Few things are more coveted by an upstart government than prestige; and, except military prowess, nothing confers that mysterious glamour more conspicuously than culture. (Be it noted, in passing, that the cost of running a first-rate culture is as nothing compared with that of half a dozen undistinguished campaigns.) Wherefore one of the earlier preoccupations of most usurped tyrannies is to patronize art and science and encourage the growth of cultivated society. The example of both Napoleons will be present to all minds, and in most there will be some recollection of the Augustan age and its eponymous chief. Such civilization as Rome did achieve, she achieved under the earlier emperors, of whom the most efficient, as a means, was that typical military despot Hadrian. The great conquerors, Cyrus, Alexander, Charlemagne, Timour, Akbar, appear all to have had a snobbish belief in culture; and it needed only a short period of gestation for the successors of the prophet and of Genghis Khan to become the Prince Consorts, if not the Medici, of their empires. Certain it is that sweetness and light have often radiated from the courts of tyrants and usurpers; for though for creative artists rulers can do little directly beyond giving them the benefits of order and security and leaving them alone, for civilization they can do much. They can endow and defend a civilizing class. That is why I think of sending copies of this essay to the Russian 'bosses,' to Signor Mussolini, and to Mr. Winston Churchill."

Bierce rarely had occasion to write about international politics. Most of his active newspaper work was done before the period when such matters became of any interest to the American people. Nevertheless, what little he did have to say is of some interest for the light that it casts on his way of thinking. As with most matters to which he turned his attention, his views were markedly realistic.

Of the foreign nations about which he had occasion to express an opinion France and England stood highest in his regard. He admired the wit of the French. He admired everything about the English. His Anglomania has been commented on before. It was his opinion that: "The American eulogist of civilization who is not proud of his heritage in England's glory is unworthy to enjoy his lesser heritage in the lesser glory of his own

235

country. . . . The English are undoubtedly our intellectual superiors; and as the virtues are solely the product of intelligence and cultivation—a rogue being only a dunce considered from another point of view—they are our moral superiors likewise." It seems to me, however, that he never made a more penetrating observation in the international field than this one on the Balkans: "All languages are spoken in Hell, but chiefly those of Southeastern Europe."

As he saw national politics as nothing more than a conflict of interests, so he considered international politics as nothing more than the same thing on a larger scale. To the usual weapons of blather and inside deals the contenders in the international field added the use of armed force. War was the instrument used to rectify national frontiers and to gain the usually unjust ends of national policy. If two nations made a treaty they simply had their hands so deeply in each other's pockets that they couldn't conveniently be parted.

Once combined, they usually used their united strength to plunder a third party. Skeptical as always, he disposed of international arbitration as follows: "International arbitration may be defined as the substitution of many burning questions for a smouldering one."

His long residence on the Pacific Coast made it natural for him to take an interest in the racial problems of the Pacific Basin. He was certainly among the first to point out the folly of hoping permanently to solve the problem of Asiatic immigration by exclusion laws alone. He recognized that with astonishing blindness the European powers were teaching the Asiatic peoples the art of war—that they were preparing the Asiatics to take up arms against the Europeans. He saw, too, that the adoption of European armaments and other Western forms of social organization was retrogression for China and Japan, but that the new armies and navies gave them political consequence in the world. He predicted in 1890 that the time would come when China

and Japan would assert their rights and force
the United States and the other powers to
concede them the status of all other first-
class powers including the freedom of move-
ment of their nationals. When that day came
he felt that it would not be long before war
would follow. He recognized that once they
fully understood and utilized Western technique in war and otherwise they would not
long accept quietly the status of inferiors.

It is extremely unfortunate that Bierce's
comments on international matters were so
rare and fragmentary. Once again it is necessary to complain that lack of an audience
kept him from giving full utterance to his
thoughts and observations.

Chapter 4

RELIGION

BIERCE professed ignorance of theology but an understanding of religion. But on no subject was he more circumspect in professing his opinions publicly. In a letter he wrote, flatly enough, "I loathe religions, a Christian gives me qualms and a Catholic sets my teeth on edge. . . ." Not only are his publicly avowed opinions phrased with exceeding care, but they are also written in a more tolerant spirit than his excursions into other fields of controversy.

He believed that religion was a matter of the heart, and as a man whose whole life was supposed to be dominated by the head, Bierce viewed it with suspicion. Nothing seemed to him more destructive of religion than logic and a sense of the ludicrous, and he possessed

both to a superlative degree. Nothing he had
to say, however, shows that he used any other
weapons to defend his agnosticism. In this
field, as in the others where he was a dissident
voice, learning does not seem to have assisted
him to his conclusions. Religion he bluntly
defined as "A daughter of Hope and Fear, explaining to Ignorance the nature of the Un-
knowable." What else is it?

With all his apparent modernity, however,
Bierce was an old-fashioned man. He was a
stern, dogmatic moralist—an iconoclast of
the pre-Nietzschean variety. Nothing more
clearly illustrates this than his adulation of
Christ. The Christ Cult numbers many adherents among the anti-Christians, for they
recognize that formal Christianity does not
stem from Christ at all but from a Græco-
Roman syncretism. They recognize, too, that
Christ's principles were debased by St. Paul.
There are few American writers of fame who
have dissented from the Christ Cult, however
much they may have dissented from Chris-

tianity. One of the most famous to do so was Ralph Waldo Emerson, who wrote: "You affirm that the moral development contains all the intellectual, and that Jesus was the perfect man. I bow in reverence unfeigned before that benign man. I know more, hope more, am more, because he has lived. But if you tell me that in your opinion he has fulfilled all the conditions of man's existence, carried out to the utmost, at least by implication, all man's powers, I suspend my assent. I do not see in him cheerfulness; I do not see in him the love of natural science: I see in him no kindness for art; I see in him nothing of Socrates, of Laplace, of Shakspear. The perfect man should remind us of all great men. Do you ask me if I would rather resemble Jesus than any other man? If I should say Yes, I should suspect myself of superstition."[2]

It has already been pointed out that Bierce, perhaps laughing wryly, invoked the Golden Rule as a way to settle the industrial conflict.

[2] *Journal,* III, 518.

There is no doubt at all about his seriousness in praising Christ. He wrote: "This is my ultimate and determining test of right—'What, in the circumstances, would Jesus have done?' —the Jesus of the New Testament, not the Jesus of the commentators, theologians, priests and parsons. The test is perhaps not infallible, but it is exceedingly simple and gives as good practical results as any. I am not a Christian, but so far as I know, the best and truest and sweetest character in literature, next to Buddha, is Jesus Christ. He taught nothing new in goodness, for all goodness was ages old before he came; but with an almost infallible intuition he applied to life and conduct the entire law of righteousness. He was a moral lightning calculator: to his luminous intelligence the statement of the problem carried the solution—he could not hesitate, he seldom erred. That upon his deeds and words was founded a religion which in a debased form persists and even spreads to this day is attestation of his marvellous gift: adoration is merely a primitive form of approval. . . . It seems a pity that this wonderful man had not a longer life under more complex conditions —conditions more nearly resembling those of the modern world and the future. One would like to be able to see, through the eyes of his biographers, his genius applied to more and other difficult questions. Yet one can hardly go wrong in inference of his thought and act. In many of the complexities and entanglements of modern affairs it is no easy matter to find an answer off-hand to the question, 'What is it right to do?' But put it in another way: 'What would Christ have done?' and lo! there is light! Doubt spreads her bat-like wings and is away; the sun of truth springs into the sky, splendoring the path of right and masking that of wrong with a deeper shade."

Now when considered in relation to his other opinions, this is extremely astonishing. To my mind it clearly shows that Bierce never even started to synthesize his opinions, otherwise he would never have placed this moral stumbling block in the centre of his system. It is utterly impossible to reconcile his Christ morality with his advocacy of an aristocratic organization of society. Even if we did not have in mind Nietzsche's contention that Christianity is a slave morality this would still be apparent. By adulating Christ, Bierce hoisted himself on the horns of a dilemma. Which would he follow when the showdown came, the aristocratic morality necessary for the establishment and preservation of his politico-economic system? or the Christ morality that his heart led him to approve? Further to make apparent the anomaly of Bierce's Christ adulation, we may cite his "this worldliness" and his denial of immortality.

This is as good a place as any to emphasize another proof that Bierce was old-fashioned. In dealing with his column, "Prattle," it was pointed out that his attacks on individuals were dictated by his high moral code. He placed great emphasis on such concepts as

honour and gentlemanliness. Now one can
hardly disapprove of this, but one may justly
object to the severe dogmatism that charac-
acterized Bierce's judgments. He never for
one moment saw that acts are not moral or
immoral in themselves, but only become so
by the attitude of the observer. He never even
suspected the truth of Nietzsche's epigram:
"There is no such thing as moral phenomena,
but only a moral interpretation of phenomena." His dogmatism. places him not among
the free spirits of the world, but in a class with
the moralists, high and low, who can see nothing but sin in any deviations from their narrow codes. He was a Puritan who had changed
his coat. Even his belief in the general worth-
lessness of the masses was closer to the doctrine
of original sin than to the modern distrust,
which is based on the findings of differential
and herd psychology.

Since the parentage of *The Monk and the
Hangman's Daughter* is under a cloud I have

reserved it for consideration here under the heading of "Religion." How much Bierce read into the story it is impossible to tell. With a somewhat natural prejudice in his favour I am inclined to believe that he brought out the essential dramatic conflict much more forcibly than it would have appeared under a lesser hand. Furthermore, it seems likely to me that he had more than a little to do with making the book so flawless an example of style. The style of *The Monk* is simple and direct. There are no passages of tortuous analysis, nor any of mere rhetoric, two flaws that burden most literary excursions into religious psychology.

Fiction dealing with religion has been a more or less constant phenomenon in American literature, but the products have been relatively unimportant. The earliest example with which I am acquainted is William Wirt's *The Blind Preacher*, of 1803. It is from predominantly Catholic countries that most of the best religious fiction comes. In those countries it is usually the product of a reaction against religion. It is also notable that whether a writer of religious fiction is Catholic or not, he is, if his book is of a superior sort, pretty sure to be a non-religious person. Orthodox writers rarely produce fictional studies of religion that have any value. The same is true of avowedly atheistic writers. It is only when the religious passions have cooled off a bit that fictional studies of religious conduct are made possible. In spite of the fact that the United States has been highly religious and has indeed been prolific in the production of minor sects and aberrations, American religious fiction has been of a very low quality. This would seem to prove the foregoing generalizations. It is notable, too, that the contemporary interest in fictional studies of religious behaviour has come during a period in which religion has ceased to be a serious concern of the intellectual classes. We may expect our best novels of religion in the future.

To my knowledge there is only one other

novel dealing with religion, written by an American before 1900, that compares with Bierce's *Monk*. That novel is Harold Frederic's *The Damnation of Theron Ware*. The two are only comparable in that they deal with religious phenomena. *The Damnation* is set in central New York State and has for its subject the intellectual and emotional struggles of a sincere if somewhat limited Methodist preacher, who, irritated by the tawdriness of the evangelists who come to stir up a revival in his community, is seduced from Methodist orthodoxy by the Catholics with whom he comes in contact. He abandons his church to start life anew and, unable to satisfy his vague intellectual and emotional stirrings in a more elevated manner, seeks an outlet for his talents in politics.

Bierce's *Monk* has quite another setting and quite another conflict. The drama takes place in the year 1680 in and about "the Monastery of Berchtesgaden, near Salzburg." The conflict centres about the calls of earthly love and religious aspirations. The narrator and central figure in the story is the monk, Ambrosius, twenty-one years of age. He has been sent from Passau by his superior to complete his novitiate at Berchtesgaden. If he is successful in meeting the demands of the religious life he will be anointed a priest. It is the first time that Ambrosius and his companions have seen mountains, and their awe at them and delight in them provide an adequate setting for the dramatic conflict that is to follow. In figuring the mountains to the reader Bierce exploits to the full his gift for rendering natural scenery that so impressed Arnold Bennett. Bennett believes that Bierce had a unique feeling for landscape. The isolation of the mountains also provided the abstraction from ordinary life which was so necessary before Bierce could enter into the spirit of the narrative. *The Monk* perfectly answers his definition of a romance.

On their way to the monastery Ambrosius and his companions chance to see a beautiful young girl scaring birds of prey away from a corpse hanging on a gallows. Ambrosius's companions are moved to break their journey and pray for the repose of the soul of the unfortunate man, but Ambrosius is more moved to discover the identity of the girl who takes her unpleasant task so nonchalantly. He discovers her to be the hangman's daughter, and, by the custom of the time, a social and religious outcast. Since he has not yet fully dedicated himself to the Church he is unable to compartmentalize his compassion, and, sexually stirred by the beauty of the girl, he rationalizes his intense interest in her as nothing more than solicitude for an unfortunate being. Acting on this pious assumption he attempts to extend protection and religious solace to her. He does so publicly and is promptly rebuked by his Superior. He is ordered to undergo penance. The girl climbs an almost inaccessible cliff opposite his cell and throws him rare flowers. He is torn between an unadmitted earthly love and an exquisite belief that he has won an outcast soul to God.

During the festivals that take place shortly after he witnesses with a mixture of envy and pious horror the pleasures of the populace. He discovers that the girl is the object of the perverse affection of a roistering young blade whose conquests are notorious. At the height of the drunken riot the young man decides that none other than the hangman's daughter is a fit companion for his revels. The announcement is a direct insult to his more orthodox love, who seeks an immediate revenge. She appeals to Ambrosius to save the girl by forewarning her. She leads him to the hangman's house by a shorter way than that taken by the drunken boys. The girl is found with her ailing father. She hesitates but a moment and then slips out to join the rout. Ambrosius returns to find her dancing madly in the centre of the bacchanalian crowd.

This experience brings his unavowed conflict to a higher pitch. He is jealous. Lying rumours are circulated to the effect that the girl has become the mistress of the young blade. Ambrosius rebuts them by explaining that she joined the crowd to avoid a scene in which her father might have been injured. His Superior once more summons him and takes him to task for defending an outcast. Ambrosius again undergoes penance for his folly. The conflict is made unbearable shortly after, when he witnesses the mob, directly after Mass, force the hangman to lead his daughter to the pillory loaded with the marks of a proved harlot. Ambrosius falls in a swoon and becomes seriously ill.

The nature of his conflict is now apparent to the eyes of the Superior, who sees that it is a conflict that can only be resolved by the most severe discipline. He consequently sends Ambrosius to the higher mountains to pray and struggle alone. Just as he seems to have succeeded in sublimating his sexual desires into ardent religiosity the girl appears on the scene. Her father has died, and she, unable to endure the disapproval of her neighbours, has fled. Her presence revives the conflict in a more acute manner than ever. It is further heightened by the appearance in the neighbourhood of the roistering youth whose attentions have caused the girl to be unjustly labelled a harlot.

Ambrosius encounters the youth, and they grapple in a fight to the death, Ambrosius labouring under the delusion that he is defending the girl from the unwholesome attentions of the youth, and the latter under the impression that he is defending her from the unnatural attentions of the monk. When Ambrosius's life is at the youth's disposal, the latter warns Ambrosius to go about his proper business and leaves him to recover from his wounds as best he may. Instead of crawling back to his hermitage Ambrosius hides away in the mountains. He ignores the calls of the messenger from his Superior, who is summoning him for a final examination before sending him to Passau for ordination.

When he emerges from his hiding place he

is quite unbalanced. Returning to the place
where he fought his rival he finds a dagger
that he had wrested from his opponent at the
beginning of the struggle. With this, he seeks
out the girl and finds her combing her hair
by the firelight and singing a passionate love
song of the countryside. He accuses her of
succumbing to the machinations of the youth
and warns her that she cannot hope for marriage because of the stigma under which she
labours. She replies that the youth has promised to have that taken care of. In fury Ambrosius whips out his dagger and stabs her.
He clasps her to him and allows her blood to
run down over his body.

The narrative continues: "I wrapped the
beautiful body in a white sheet, leaving the
face uncovered, and laid it upon the floor.
But the blood tinged the linen, so I parted her
long golden hair, spreading it over the crimson
roses upon her breast. As I had made her a
bride of Heaven, I took from the image of the
Virgin the wreath of edelweiss and placed it

on Benedicta's brow; and now I remembered
the edelweiss which she had once brought me
to comfort me in my penance. . . . Then I
stirred the fire, which cast upon the shrouded
figure and the beautiful face a rich red light,
as if God's glory had descended there to en-
fold her. It was caught and tangled in the golden tresses that lay upon her breast, so that
they looked a mass of curling flame. . . . And
so I left her. . . . I descended the mountain by
precipitous paths, but God guided my steps
so that I neither stumbled nor fell into the
abyss. At the dawning of the day I arrived at
the monastery, rang the bell and waited until
the gate was opened. The brother porter evidently thought me a fiend, for he raised a howl
that aroused the whole monastery. I went
straight to the room of the Superior, stood before him in my blood-stained garments, and,
telling him for what deed the Lord had chosen
me, informed him that I was now an ordained
priest. At this they seized me, put me into the
tower, and, holding court upon me, con-

demned me to death as if I were a murderer.
O, the fools, the poor demented fools!"

As has been remarked, it is impossible to
isolate Bierce's contributions to this remarkable romance, but I think it entirely logical
and just to attribute to him the clarity of
style and the skill with which the underlying
motif was brought to the attention of the
reader without being unduly obtrusive. Even
as a story the tale is most remarkable, but if
we examine it as a psychological document it
is even more extraordinary. That Bierce clearly
perceived the essentials of the sexual-psycho-
logical conflict seems to me reasonable to
assume. If this be true his insight led him to
bring out a drama that would give joy to the
heart of any Freudian. The importance of sex
as a component of religious fervour is widely
recognized to-day. It is clearly brought out
in Bierce's romance. He undoubtedly saw that
the conflict between the flesh and the devil
and the call to God would heighten Ambro-

sius's religious fervour if he could attain some degree of detachment. He also saw how easy it was for Ambrosius to sublimate his sexual desires in religious imagery. But to heighten the drama he recognized that it was not wise to carry the sublimation too far. He therefore brought the conflict from Ambrosius's subconscious to his conscious mind. Bierce then cleverly arranged the development of the action so that Ambrosius could achieve a new sublimation. But this was of a very tenuous nature. Bringing the girl once more before him would destroy it before it had a chance to become an undisturbable psychological mechanism. This done the conflict would come out in the open again. It was then logical to show that it was beyond Ambrosius's powers to resolve the conflict by renouncing his vows and marrying the girl. Bierce therefore resorted to the device of letting the religious in Ambrosius's mentality get the upper hand so completely as to unbalance him. In an unbalanced state it was logical for Ambrosius to evolve a rationalization of his murder. He was making the girl the bride of Christ. In reality he was making her his own bride. It is hardly necessary to do more than mention that a dagger and blood are sexual symbols of very obvious meaning.

PART IV
CONCLUSION

IT WAS remarked in the opening section of this book that Bierce has not yet achieved the position in American letters to which he is entitled. His reputation is still chiefly sustained by the worst sort of following an author can have: he is the god of a cult. As time goes on there is every chance that his reputation will be broadened and extended until it will be known to all those who take a serious interest in American letters. It may be doubted that he will ever achieve anything in the way of general popularity. His appeal is too narrow for that, and his substance too slight to bear the weight of such a burden. In time he will be something more than an anthology author and something less than an author whose collected works are found in every sizable library. This opinion is based on the assumption that his reputation is on the up grade. It is. Just before he died George Sterling wrote: "I regret that I may not use the forbidden metaphor, 'a star rising in the West.' None other would so well express the gathering light and slow inevitability of as- cension of Ambrose Bierce's fame. The Wise Men of the East first saw it as a feeble spark scarcely to be detected through the haze and murk of the western horizon. 'A little,' they might have said, 'and it will have set.' But a little, and it had crept a degree further up the literary heavens, and was finally visible even from Europe." But however optimistic one may be it is necessary to admit that Bierce's reputation will always be somewhat narrow and special. It will never be very wide or very inclusive.

Whether or not it will increase his reputation to make known his ideas as has been done in this monograph I do not know. It will cer- tainly contribute to making him more interest- ing. It will also help to make him understood and to make it more generally realized what extraordinary potentialities he had. When this study was undertaken it was not with the idea of presenting one more frustrated American writer to the public. The conclusion that he was frustrated is one that must be accepted after a careful study of the evidence. Even a writer approaching Bierce without prepossessions, as I believe I did, will have to recognize that it is the truth.

Admitting for the moment the entire truth of Van Wyck Brooks's analysis of Mark Twain, it is illuminating to compare him to Bierce. Bierce knew that he could have achieved popular acclaim by following contemporary fashion in art and thought. He knew that he had developed a flexible enough technical equipment to turn out stories acceptable to the popular magazines. But he refused to do so. He wrote: "I know how to write a story (of the 'happy ending' sort) for magazine readers for whom literature is too good, but I will not do so so long as stealing is more honorable and interesting." Bierce, then, saw the prob-

lem of authorship in his America with clear
eyes. He was possessed of sufficient capacity
for criticism to pose the problem and define
his conclusion. With almost unequalled fortitude he rejected the easiest way and kept faith
with himself. Bierce was an extremely self-
conscious man—sometimes too self-conscious.
Mark Twain, on the other hand, did not see
the difficulties of authorship until after he had
gone so far along the road to popular acclaim
that he could not retreat. Then and then
only did he begin to revolt against the re-
straints that he had let himself in for. In other
words, his case is Bierce's reversed. Bierce
saw the inevitable result of making concessions
before he was tempted to make any. Twain
saw the results of making concessions after
they were made. Bierce was outspoken from
the very beginning of his career. He started
to print bits of what later became *The Devil's
Dictionary* in 1881. Mark Twain reserved what
he thought were his choicest reflections on the
human race until after his death. Who can

imagine Bierce writing, as Mark Twain did, this astonishing prefatory note to his unexciting *Autobiography:* "I am writing from the grave. On these terms only can a man be approximately frank. He cannot be straitly and unqualifiedly frank either in the grave or out of it." This opinion Bierce would have denied without qualification.

Of course it is not possible for one moment to compare Mark Twain and Bierce as to the quality of their intellects. It is almost beyond question that Bierce's mind was keener, more disciplined, more penetrating, and in every way of a higher quality. If their cynicisms run parallel it is because they were both underfed intellectually and both betray a lack of culture. But the quality of their minds was quite different, and the potentialities of Bierce impress me much more than those of Mark Twain.

Yet in the bulk of work actually done, the fact remains that Mark Twain is far ahead of Bierce. In the final reckoning Mark Twain is an infinitely more important writer than Bierce. This may, perhaps, be attributed to the fact that Mark Twain was gifted with a greater creative capacity than Bierce, and creation has little to do with incisiveness of intellect. Nevertheless, it is very remarkable indeed that the two men can be so instructively compared.

It has been suggested earlier that Bierce was frustrated by rejection and William Dean Howells by acceptance. Mark Twain's name may be substituted for that of Howells without disturbing the truth of the generalization. It seems to me that it is worth while to re-emphasize my opinion that Bierce was not frustrated as a writer by any personal inadequacy. Neither was he frustrated by any personal restraint placed upon him. Even in writing journalism for Hearst he was put under no restraint by Hearst himself. Bierce said what he pleased. Even when Bierce wrote the verse about the assassin of Goebel, Governor of Kentucky:

BITTER BIERCE

The bullet that pierced Goebel's breast
Can not be found in all the West.
Good reason: it is speeding here
To stretch McKinley on the bier—

which was later distorted by Hearst's enemies
into the accusation that he had prior knowledge that McKinley was to be assassinated,
if, indeed, he did not encourage the fanatic to
attack the President, Hearst said nothing to
Bierce. In later years Hearst's subordinates
made trouble for Bierce, but when that time
came Bierce was at the end of his career and
quite ready to quit. Bierce was frustrated by
his environment—by his parish and his time.
I do not think that his writings have a local
reference simply because he was not capable
of attaining a national point of view. He
wrote about local happenings because he was
writing for a local audience. His frustration
came as a result of his inability to achieve an
audience sufficiently large and of sufficiently
high a quality to bring out the best in him.
Bierce was not the sort of man to be inter-

ested in writing for itself, to expand and elaborate his ideas unless he felt that there was an audience waiting for his books. The consequence was that he brought none of his ideas into a conclusive form, and when he set about assembling his collected edition he had nothing to work with but essays the edge of which had worn off and which half expressed his meaning. For that reason about eight volumes of the twelve will never be read except by students. It is only when we approach Bierce from this angle that we discover that he was frustrated.

Another way in which his environment had a direct effect on him is in the matter of his cultural equipment. Since he never felt the urge to carry his thoughts to conclusive form, he never felt any desire to elaborate his scholarship to a scale commensurate with the penetration of his thinking. This left him only half prepared to sustain his argumentation. It seems to me here as before that if Bierce had felt a public was awaiting his work he would have repaired the gaps in his learning with ease and pleasure.

From all this it is apparent that I do not think that Bierce was essentially a man of letters. If he had been he would not have let his chance to leave an important body of work behind him escape. He was essentially a man of action who chose to function in letters. He needed something to fight against to arouse his best powers. The mere act of composition gave him small satisfaction. It has been remarked before, that in spite of his worship of his particular manner of expression, he apparently did not find pleasure in working with words. He was not an artist in words the way Walter Pater was, for instance. He regarded his skill in expression in the same way that a swordsman regards his skill with the rapier. It was a convenient weapon with which to dispose of the fools and rogues he disliked.

In spite of all these reservations it is still possible to regard Bierce as one of the most

important writers of his day and a significant
figure in American literature. He stands out
from every other writer of his generation for
his independence, for the fact that he spoke
out in meeting in no uncertain terms, and for
the originality of his thinking. Mr. Lewis
Mumford has pointed out that the period between 1870 and 1900 was as a whole a dark
period in the history of the American mind,
but that during the same period there were
strange burgeonings of the future. Ambrose
Bierce must be regarded as one of the writers
who gave some indication of what was coming.

If we name over the writers of his day that
dominated the literary scene we shall see two
things: first, that he was at variance with
them on almost every point, and second, that
he is marked off from them by his modernity.
Of course this modernity was not in the field
of literature. In that field his theories were
heretical enough but not modern. The same
generalization may be made about his stories

themselves, inevitable products of his theories as they are. But his attitude toward the literary life was so high and for its realization demanded such boundless freedom that it must be denominated modern in so far as the United States is concerned. He fought for the freedom of the writer from every sort of environmental restriction. It is true that he went a bit too far and set out a programme that would not only have insured freedom but would have deracinated the writer, but the important thing is that he demanded freedom. It is also true that he placed too little emphasis on the importance of environmental pressure as a factor in determining the complexion of a writer's opinions. But these limitations sink into insignificance before the fact that he saw that the greatest limitation on authorship in America was the lack of a demand for independence on the part of the writers themselves.

It was in the field of ideas that we must concede the rôle of forerunner without too many reservations. The ideas he entertained are now accepted by dozens of modern writers, most of whom required the catastrophe of the World War to bring them to their conclusions. The essential and differentiating difference between Bierce and the general run of contemporary thinkers is that he had an old-fashioned attitude toward morals. He still followed a rigid code and judged the validity of men and social conduct by their conformance to or deviation from it. This strikes us as old-fashioned. We are a bit alienated by his positiveness. We have a greater feeling for the relativity of all ideas. But our greater latitudinarianism should not blind us to the essential modernity of the ideas that Bierce evolved.

In the face of all the considerations that can be brought forth for calling Bierce a forerunner of the modern age, it is idle any longer to deny him a permanent place in the American literary hierarchy. He is certainly more worthy of a place than such writers as Bret Harte, O. Henry, James Whitcomb Riley,

George Ade, and a host of other minor writers whose names inevitably appear in every survey of American literature. It must be conceded that he is worthy of a place along with Frank Norris, Stephen Crane, and Jack London, who, in spite of their foibles and failures, are reckoned to have been writers of high merit. He, like these, had a part in the coming of age of American literature.

NOTE

BIERCE's chief books were published as follows:

Tales of Soldiers and Civilians. E. L. G. Steele, San Francisco, 1891 (reissued, New York, 1898, as *In the Midst of Life*).

The Monk and the Hangman's Daughter. F. J. Schulte & Company, Chicago, 1892.

Can Such Things Be? Caffell Publishing Company, New York, 1893.

The Cynic's Word Book. Doubleday, Page & Company, New York, 1906. (Later the original title was restored, *The Devil's Dictionary*.)

Collected Works (in twelve volumes). Neale Publishing Company, New York and Washington, 1909–1912.

Four of Bierce's books are in The American Library published by Albert and Charles Boni, Inc., apparently printed from the plates of the *Collected Works: In the*

BITTER BIERCE

Midst of Life, The Monk and the Hangman's Daughter (also in this volume is a collection of fables), *Can Such Things Be?*, and *The Devil's Dictionary.*

In the Midst of Life is also available in The Modern Library with a preface by George Sterling.

In England *In the Midst of Life, Can Such Things Be?*, *The Monk and the Hangman's Daughter*, and *The Devil's Dictionary* can be obtained in Jonathan Cape's *Travellers' Library.*

INDEX

INDEX

Adams, F. P., 193.

Adams, John, Bierce's political agreement with, 226.

Ade, George, 5.

Aldrich, Thomas Bailey, his place in the evolution of the short story, 129; his style compared with that of Bierce, 130.

Ambrose Bierce, quotation from, 75–76 and *footnote* 76.

"Ambrose Bierce as He Really Was," *footnote* 83.

American, New York, Bierce is attached to the Washington Bureau of the, 69–70.

American and British Literature Since 1890, 5.

American Literature Since 1870, 6.

American Mercury, 14; quotation from George Sterling in the, 17 and *footnote;* comment on Bierce and Aldrich in the, 130.

American Parade, footnote 83.

"Another Way," 192.

Argonaut, Bierce contributes regularly to the, 43 and *footnote.*

Aristotle, 125.

Athenæum, London, a comment on Bierce in the, 37.

Atlantic Monthly, 17.

Autobiography, quotation from preface of Mark Twain's, 265.

Bacon, Sir Francis, the subject of *Novum Organum,* 35.

Barnes, Harry Elmer, 218.

Bat, The, Bierce a contributor to, 29.

Beer, Thomas, 133; his summary of war as a subject for great fiction, 137.

Bell, Clive, *Civilization* quoted, 233.

Bennett, Arnold, his comment on Bierce's reputation, 8; his belief that journalism was harmful to Bierce's literary contributions, 99; points out Bierce's feeling for landscape, 249.

Bierce, Abigail, 13.

Bierce, Albert, the relationship between Ambrose and, 12; his feeling that the war matured his brother, 14; comments on wound Ambrose received at Kenesaw Mountain, 17; Ambrose considers joining him in San Francisco, 18; the break between Ambrose and, 76.

Bierce, Ambrose. Part I: Biography. His war with an oppressive environment, 3; his position in American letters, 5–8; Dr. F. L. Pattee's judgment of, 6; his life summarized in comparison with that of

279

INDEX

William Dean Howells, 8–10; parentage and family, 10–13; boyhood, 13; war experience, 14–18; goes to Alabama as official of the Treasury Department, 18; crosses plains to California in engineering capacity, 19; is employed in mint with his brother, 20; contributes to newspapers and is appointed editor of the *News-Letter*, 20; his marriage, 21–23; begins literary work seriously in London, 23; his contributions to *Fun*, the *Comic Annual*, and other humorous publications, 26–29; first books appear, 24; is given *The Lantern* to edit, 31; he ridicules Henri de Rochefort, 31–36; declines invitation to visit the Empress, 36; his life in London 36 ff.; a trip to Paris, *footnote* 38; returns in 1876 to San Francisco, 38; his appearance and personal characteristics, 39–42; incident which resulted in his suffering from asthma, 42; contributes to the *Wasp*, *Argonaut*, and occasional other papers, 43; hired by W. R. Hearst in 1881, 43; his dictatorship in San Francisco, 43 ff.; his comment upon Stephen Crane's, *The Red Badge of Courage*, 45; his literary influence, 46; contacts with writers, 47–52; he meets Jack London, 47; a congenial acquaintance with Percival Pollard, 50–51; Mrs. J. C. McCrackin recalls

his summer in the Santa Cruz mountains, 53; his relations with women, 52–55 and *footnote* 55; is engaged in 1910, 54–55; he manages briefly a gold mine in South Dakota, 55; establishes his famous column, "Prattle," in the San Francisco *Examiner*, 56 ff.; his method of satirical attack, 57–60; ethical philosophy, 59; apologizes to George Sterling for the character of "Prattle," 61; the 'nineties the period of his greatest contributions to literature, 61 ff.; the publication of *Tales of Soldiers and Civilians*, 62; contemporary and present-day judgments of his work, 62; early struggles for recognition, 62; *The Monk and the Hangman's Daughter* appears and arouses controversy, 62–66; the publications of *Can Such Things Be?* *Black Beetles in Amber*, *Fantastic Fables*, *Shapes of Clay*, *The Cynic's Word Book*, *Write it Right*, and *The Shadow on the Dial and Other Essays*, 66–67; goes to Washington, 68; the controversy with Collis P. Huntington, 68 and *footnote;* is attached to the Washington Bureau of the New York *American*, 69–70; conducts "The Passing Show" in the *Cosmopolitan*, 69–70; his relations with Hearst, 70–71; gives up newspaper writing in 1909, 72; collected works ap-

INDEX

pear between 1909 and 1912, 72; a period of dissatisfaction, 73; the death of his son Leigh, 73-74; in 1913 plans trip to Mexico and perhaps to South America, 74; farewell letters to Mrs. J. C. McCrackin, 75; visits battlefields of the South, 76-80; last knowledge of him in Chihuahua, Mexico, 80; contradictory reports of his disappearance and death, 80-84; the anecdote of himself told to Ruth Guthrie Harding, 84; his contradictory character, 85 ff.; writes Sterling his opinion on the serenity of genius, 87; the nature of his audience, 91; his opposition to popular dogma, 92; replies to a contemporary journalist who accuses him of being embittered by failure, 94; comments upon literary conditions in Ug, 94; the cynic, 95. Part II: Literature. The effect of journalism upon his work, 99; literary theories and ideals, 100 ff.; his estimate of contemporary literature, 101; his thesis against publishers, 102-109; his opinions on literature with a "purpose," local colour and dialect, slang, 109-113; on the novel, 113-115; his dislike of realism, 115; ideas on poetry, 115-116; an explanation of the small contemporary audience he attracted, 116-117; literary preferences, 118; his formula for training a

writer, 118-120; essentials of the literary art, 121; the topics with which he dealt, 121; his philosophy of the short story, 121; critical powers, 123-124; influences responsible for his ideas on art, 124-126; the extent of his culture, 126-127; his knowledge of the theatre, music, painting, economics, sociology, politics, 127-128; his style compared with Aldrich's, 130; his link with O. Henry and Bret Harte, 131; the one connection he had with contemporary trends, 131; O. Henry and Stephen Crane influenced by, 132; the question of his "influence," 133; war stories, 134 ff.; the war as a congenial subject, 135; in 1892 publishes *Tales of Soldiers and Civilians*, 138; his view of war, 138-143; his ideal of the soldier, 141; the war stories summarized, 143 ff.; an analysis of "One of the Missing," 145 ff.; stories of the supernatural, 152 ff.; themes which attracted his imagination, 154-156; "a Jug of Sirup" analyzed, 156 ff.; characteristics of his ghost stories, 161; "The Damned Thing" analyzed, 164 ff.; an analysis of "The Death of Halpin Frayser," 170 ff.; "Moxon's Master" reviewed, 174 ff.; the satirist and wit, 184 ff.; his ideas of wit, 186; examples of his wit, 187-189; the poet, 190 ff.;

281

INDEX

his judgment of his poetic abilities, 191; best poems in the opinion of George Sterling, 192; as a writer of *vers de société*, 193; invectives in verse, 194. Part III: Ideas. On man and life, 199; on woman, 203; his philosophy applied to his own life, 205 ff.; advocate of selective breeding of human beings, 208; prison reform measures, 210; the good life, 212; the capitalistic system, 214; contemporary commerce, 215; exploitation, 216; unemployment, 218; a defender of trusts, 219; labour unions and labour leaders, 220; capitalism, 223; an enemy of democracy, 224; the political ideal, 225; his associates in political thought, 226; an "aristocratic radical," 227; his criticism of democracy, 228; a programme of government, 231–232; Clive Bell in political harmony with, 233; internationalism, 235–238; religious beliefs, 239 ff.; definition of religion, 240; his Christ morality, 240–244; a Puritan, 245; *The Monk and the Hangman's Daughter* analyzed as religious fiction, 245 ff. Part IV: Conclusion. His position in American letters, 261; compared with Mark Twain, 263–266; frustration, 266–268; cultural equipment, 268; a man of action functioning in letters, 269; summary of his period and theories, 270–271;

his superiority, 271; his place among his contemporaries, 272–273; his chief books listed, 274–275.

Bierce, Andrew, 13; Ambrose visits his farm, 18.

Bierce, Day, 21.

Bierce, Frederick, 11.

Bierce, Helen, *see* Isgrigg, Mrs. Helen Bierce.

Bierce, Laura Sherwood, 10.

Bierce, Leigh, his character, 21–22; "John Mortonson's Funeral" a memorial to, *footnote*, 22; his death in 1901, 73–74.

Bierce, Marcus Aurelius, 10; the character of, and his relations with his son, 11.

Bierce, Mrs. M. A., tells of seeing Ambrose for the last time, 18.

Bierce, Mollie Day, her marriage to Ambrose Bierce, 21.

Bierce, Colonel Royal C., 11.

Biglow Papers, The, 111.

Billings, Josh, 186.

"Bits of Autobiography," *footnote*, 20; *footnote* 36.

Black Beetles in Amber, its publication in 1895, 67; Bierce's explanation of, 191.

Blind Preacher, The, 246.

Boni, A. & C., Inc., *footnote* 36; 274.

Bookman, quotation from article on Bierce quoted in the *footnote*, 8; *footnote* 74; essay on Bierce by Wilson Follette in the, *footnote* 185.

Bookman, London, Walter Jerrold's article, "The Identity of Dod Grile," in the, *footnote*, 26.

282

INDEX

INDEX

INDEX

"For the Ahkoond," 133.
Ford, Henry, 216.
F. P. A., 193.
Frederic, Harold, theme of his *The Damnation of Theron Ware*, 248.
Freeman, Mary Wilkins, 111.
French, Joseph Lewis, gives exposition of Bierce's literary position in San Francisco, 44; speaks of Bierce as "old Presbyterian," 208.
Fun, Bierce is associated with the literary group centring about, 23 ff.
Funston, General, his failure to gain knowledge of Bierce's whereabouts, 81.

Garland, Hamlin, contrasted with Bierce as a critic of his environment, 3; 111.
"Geotheas," quoted, 192–193.
Gilbert, W. S., his association with Bierce and the group centring about *Fun*, 24; title page of *The Fiend's Delight* illustrated by, 25.
Glanvill, 126.
Goebel, Governor of Kentucky, Bierce's verse on, 266–267.
Goethe, 101, 126.
Grousset, M. Pascal, accompanies Henri de Rochefort on his arrival in England, 33.
Guedalla, Philip, describes Henri de Rochefort in *The Second Empire*, 29.

Hamilton, Alexander, Bierce's political agreement with, 226.

Hamilton, E. H., *footnote, 20; footnote 21*.
Hamilton, Judge Noble, Bierce is married at the home of, 21.
Harding, Ruth Guthrie, her article on Bierce quoted, *footnote 8; footnote 74*; her anecdote of Bierce, 84.
Hardy, Thomas, 7.
Harte, Bret, contrasted with Bierce as a critic of his environment, 3; 24; his place in the evolution of the short story, 129; the point of contact between his work and Bierce's, 131; his place in relation to Bierce, 272.
Hawthorne, Nathaniel, 113, 127; his use of the supernatural theme in literature, 153.
Hay, John, 24.
Hazen, General W. B., Bierce attached to the staff of, 16; Bierce with Western expedition under, 19.
Hearn, Lafcadio, his early use of the supernatural in literature, 153–154; quotes remark of Scott relative to the appeal of the supernatural, 183.
Hearst, William Randolph, hires Bierce for the *Examiner*, 43; engages Bierce to contribute a Sunday feature article to the *Examiner*, 56; sends Bierce to Washington in Huntington controversy over the railroads, 68; Bierce's relations with, 70–71; Bierce independent of, 266–267.
Heine, 126.

INDEX

Henry, O., 5; his place in the evolution of the short story, 129; his link with Bierce, 131; the influence of Bierce upon, 132; his position in relation to Bierce, 272.

Hill, W. M., Chicago, *footnote* 76.

Homer, 126.

Hood, Tom, editor of *Fun*, 24.

Horace, 126.

"Horseman in the Sky, A," contrasted with Aldrich's "White Feather," 130; its place among Bierce's war stories, 144.

Hortense, Queen, 30.

Hotten, John Camden, Bierce's relations with, 24–26; Bierce's protest to, regarding the publication of *The Fiend's Delight*, 28.

Hovey, Richard, 5.

"How I Came to Like Dogs," Bierce's first contribution to Tom Hood's *Comic Annual*, 27.

Howells, W. D., contrasted with Bierce as a critic of his environment, 3; Bierce compared with, 8–10; "Miss Nancy Howells," 129; his feeling about war as a hostile influence for the artist, 136; 147; 266.

Huckleberry Finn, its expression of protest, 3.

Hugo, Victor, 114, 126.

Huntington, Collis P., his controversy with the government relative to a settlement of $75,000,000, 68; 216.

"Identity of Dod Grile, The," article by Walter Jerrold in the London *Bookman*, *footnote*, 26.

"Impostor, An," quoted, 194.

In the Midst of Life, *footnote*, 52; appears in 1891 as *Tales of Soldiers and Civilians*, 62; Preface to, *footnote* 82; *footnote* 83; war stories contained in, 143; 274–275.

"Invocation," 192.

Irving, Washington, his literary use of the supernatural theme, 153.

Irwin, Will, 50.

Isgrigg, Mrs. Helen Bierce, 21; makes effort to solve mystery of her father's disappearance, 84.

James, George Wharton, *footnote* 54.

James, Henry, contrasted with Bierce as a critic of his environment, 3; "Miss Nancy James" Bierce, 129.

James, William, his critical attitude toward his environment contrasted with that of Bierce, 3.

Jerrold, Walter, *footnote*, 26.

"John Mortonson's Funeral," a memorial to Leigh Bierce, *footnote*, 22.

Journal, Emerson quoted from, 241 and *footnote*.

Journal of Arthur Sterling, The, Bierce's reaction to, 87

"Jug of Sirup, A," an analysis of, 156 ff.

Juvenal, 126.

286

INDEX

Keats, 126.

Kitchener, Lord, report that Bierce was associated during the war with, 81.

Landor, Walter Savage, 125.

Lane, Franklin K., his opinion of Ambrose Bierce, 60.

Lanier, Sidney, contrasted with Bierce as a critic of his environment, 3.

Lanterne, La, Henri de Rochefort publishes it in 1868, 29; Bierce given charge of, 31; Bierce summarizes the character of, 32–35.

Letters of Ambrose Bierce, footnote 12; *footnote* 80.

Life on the Mississippi, its expression of protest, 3.

London, Jack, 42; Bierce's literary position in relation to, 273.

Longfellow, William Wadsworth, 127.

Longinus, 124, 125.

Loveman, Samuel, 50.

Lowell, James Russell, 137.

McCrackin, Mr., 54.

McCrackin, Mrs. J. C., recalls her acquaintance with Bierce, 53–54 and *footnote* 54; Bierce's farewell letters to her in 1913, 75.

McEwen, Arthur, names Bierce "Almighty God Bierce," 10.

"Mad World, A," a reference to W. R. Hearst in, 70–71.

"Man With the Hoe, The," Bierce and Markham disagree over, 47.

Markham, Edwin, disagreement between Bierce and, 47.

Mather, Cotton, 153.

Matthews, his position in the evolution of the short story, 129.

May, Boone, 56.

Melero, Dr. Edmund, claimed intimate acquaintance with Bierce in Mexico, 81.

"Memoirs of C. G. Yellowplush," 27.

Mencken, H. L., 50; his meeting with Bierce, 51; his opinion of Bierce as a wit, 184; on capitalism, 214; his agreement with Bierce, 219, 226.

Millard, 70.

Miller, Joaquin, 49; works dedicated to Collis P. Huntington, 68.

Milton, 126.

Molière, 101.

Monk and the Hangman's Daughter, The, the controversy over, 62–66; an analysis of, 245 ff.; 274–275.

Moody, Vaughn, contrasted with Bierce as a critic of his environment, 3.

More Contemporary Americans, 6.

Morrow, William C., 45.

Morryster, 126.

Mortimer, James, Bierce's association with, 29; determines character of the journal, *The Lantern* 32; approves policy of paper and directs publication of second number, 35; Bierce is given through him an invitation to visit the Empress, 36.

287

INDEX

Most, Johan, 70.

"Moxon's Master," themes of *R. U. R.* found in, Mr. Patridge asserts, 133; an analysis of, 156, 174 ff.

"Mr. Boythorn-Bierce," an article in the *Bookman* by Ruth Guthrie Harding, *footnote* 8; excerpt from article, 74 and *footnote*.

Mumford, Lewis, summary of period 1870-1900, 270.

Murfree, Mary, 111.

Mysterious Stranger, The, a protest against environment, 3.

Nasby, Petroleum V., 186.

Neale Publishing Company of Washington and New York, publishers of a collected edition of Bierce's work, 67, 274.

"Negligible Tales," "The Famous Gilson Bequest" included among, 131.

Nietzsche, 227, 244, 245.

News-Letter, Bierce is appointed editor of the, 20; *footnote* 43.

Norris, Frank, contrasted with Bierce as a critic of his environment, 3; Bierce's position in relation to, 273.

"Not Guilty," quoted, 193.

Novum Organum, quoted, 35.

Nuggets and Dust, its appearance in England, 24.

Nye, Bill, 186.

O'Brien, Edward, 129.

O'Brien, Fitz-James, his use of the supernatural in literature, 153; his "What Was It?" related to Bierce's "The Damned Thing," 164.

O'Brien, John F., quoted in *footnote* 15.

"Occurrence at Owl Creek Bridge, An," example of the "snap ending," 129; its place among Bierce's war stories, 144.

Omar Khayyâm, 126.

"One of the Missing," an analysis of, 144 ff.

O'Reilly, "Tex," his story of finding Bierce's grave, 83.

"Papyrus, The," 51.

"Passing Show, The," Bierce conducts department in the *Cosmopolitan,* 69-70.

Pater, Walter, 269.

Patridge, Eric, 126; believes Bierce influenced Capek, 133.

Pattee, Dr., his judgment of Bierce, 6; points out Bierce's contribution to the evolution of the short-story form, 128; points out link between Bierce and O. Henry, 131; credits Bierce with having influenced O. Henry, 132.

Phœnix, John, 186.

Plato, 126.

Poe, Edgar Allan, 116; Bierce's philosophy of the short story compared with that of, 121; his influence on Bierce, 125; his use of the supernatural in literature, 153.

Pollard, Percival, the acquain-

INDEX

tance between Bierce and him, 50; his estimate of Bierce, 99; quotation from his *Their Day in Court, footnote,* 109; discredits Bierce's views on painting, 127; his belief that *The Red Badge of Courage* owed much to Bierce, 132.

Pope, Alexander, 126.

Pope, B. C., *footnote,* 12; *footnote* 80.

"Prattle," name given to a scurrilous column in *The Lantern,* 34; Bierce's column in the San Francisco *Examiner* known as, 56 ff.; the character of, 60; quoted, *footnote* 109.

"Presentment," 192.

R. U. R., said by Patridge to be influenced by "Moxon's Master," 133.

Rabelais, 101.

Red Badge of Courage, The, Bierce's criticism of, 44–45; Percival Pollard's criticism of, 132; published in 1896, 138.

Reid, Mayne, a member of the group associated with *Fun,* 24.

"Reminded," 192.

Riley, James Whitcomb, 5, 92; his position in relation to Bierce, 272.

Rochefort, Henri de, a description of, 29; his exile and return, 30; Bierce undertakes to lampoon him, 31 ff.

"Romantic History of Josephine Clifford McCrackin." *footnote* 54.

Rouher, M., 30.

Sala, George Augustus, one of the group associated with *Fun,* 24; famous epitaph by, 26.

Schaffauer, Herman, his friendship with Ambrose Bierce, 49–50.

Schulte, F. J., *The Monk and the Hangman's Daughter* issued in 1892 through, 62–66.

Schulte, F. J., & Company, 64, 274.

Scott, Sir Walter, 113, 126; quoted on the appeal of the supernatural, 183.

Second Empire, The, description of Henri de Rochefort in, 29.

Seldes, Gilbert, his comment on Bierce, 184.

Shadow on the Dial and other Essays, The, its publication in 1909, 67.

"Shadow Maker, The," quotation from the article, 17 and *footnote.*

Shakespeare, 101, 126.

Shapes of Clay, its publication in 1903, 67; 191.

Sherwood, Laura, *see* Bierce, Laura Sherwood.

Sims, George R., his association with the group about *Fun,* 24.

Sinclair, Upton, attributes Bierce's hatred of socialism to an unfortunate romance, 21; Bierce's reaction to one of his heroes, 87.

Some Chinese Ghosts, quotation from Scott in preface of, 183.

Spencer, Herbert, 125.

Starrett, Vincent, *footnote* 76.

INDEX

INDEX

Ward, Artemus, 186.

Wasp, Bierce a contributor to the, 42 and *footnote* 43.

We, 133.

Weeks, George F., has report of Bierce in 1918, 81.

What Is Man? an expression of protest, 3.

"What Was It?" 164.

"White Feather," contrasted with Bierce's "A Horseman in the Sky," 130.

Whittier, John Greenleaf, 127.

Wilde, Oscar, 51.

Wirt, William, 246.

Woman Who Lost Him, The, 53 and *footnote* 54; 75.

Wordsworth, William, 200.

Works of Stephen Crane, The, *footnote* 46.

Write it Right, published in 1909, 67.

Zamiatin, 133.